COMPLETE BOOK OF

Illustrated
K-3
Alphabet Games

AND ACTIVITIES

COMPLETE BOOK OF
Illustrated
K-3
Alphabet Games
AND ACTIVITIES

Patricia Tyler Muncy

The Center for Applied Research in Education, Inc.
West Nyack, New York 10994

Library of Congress Cataloging in Publication Data

Muncy, Patricia Tyler
   Complete book of illustrated K-3 alphabet games
and activities.

   Bibliography: p.
   1. Reading games.   2. English language—Alphabet.
I. Title.
LB1525.56.M86   372.4'145   79-24036
ISBN 0-87628-230-3

Printed in the United States of America

ABOUT THIS BOOK
OF ALPHABET GAMES

The purpose of this book is to provide you with a wide variety of activities to reinforce instruction on letter recognition, manuscript letter formation, matching capital with lower case letters, simple alphabetical order, and letter sound relationships. Many of the activities can also be easily adapted to provide the needed practice and reinforcement in cursive letter recognition and writing.

The book includes 180 different instructional games and activities organized into the following skill sections: (1) Letter Recognition, Letter Formation, Oral Letter Sequence, (2) Alphabetical Order, (3) Matching Capital and Lower Case Letters, and (4) Letter Sound Relationships. In addition, special sections at the end of the book provide methods for helping students who have difficulty learning and retaining the letter names, and lists of commercially available teaching materials with publishers' addresses.

Each game and activity in the book is tested, complete, and ready for use. The instructions include a distinct title, statement of purpose, list of materials needed, preparation directions, and procedures for presenting the game. The procedures even suggest language for introducing the game to your students.

Many of the games also include illustrations of game components and patterns you can reproduce directly from the book. And many games are self-correcting. These games give students immediate corrective feedback on their responses and help prevent faulty learning. An asterisk beside the title of a game indicates that it is a self-correcting activity.

All of the games and activities are high interest, designed to actively involve the child in learning, and designed to truly motivate the child!

Patricia Tyler Muncy

ABOUT THE AUTHOR

Patricia Tyler Muncy, M.S. in Reading Education, has been actively involved in elementary education for 16 years. Her experience includes four years as a classroom teacher, five years as a 1–6 remedial reading teacher, and four years as a district reading supervisor.

She has also authored a variety of practical teaching/learning aids. These include a teacher aid book, *Word Puzzles* (Belmont, CA: Fearon-Pitman Pubs., 1974), an instructional game, *Froggie Alphabet Game* (Oak Lawn, IL: Ideal School Supply Co., 1976), and seven books of duplicator masters, *Word Play,* Books A and B (Dansville, NY: Instructor Curriculum Materials, 1977), *Handwriting,* Books A, B and C (Instructor Curriculum Materials, 1979), *Dictionary Skills Grades 1 & 2,* and *Dictionary Skills, Grades 5 & 6* (Instructor Curriculum Materials, forthcoming).

Mrs. Muncy is presently Reading Supervisor for the Wayne County Public Schools, seven school districts, and lives in Wooster, Ohio.

CONTENTS

1.   GAMES AND ACTIVITIES TO REINFORCE LETTER RECOGNITION,
       LETTER FORMATION, AND ORAL LETTER SEQUENCE
       (CONT.)

---

*Indicates a self-correcting activity.

1. GAMES AND ACTIVITIES TO REINFORCE LETTER RECOGNITION, LETTER FORMATION, AND ORAL LETTER SEQUENCE (CONT.)

2. GAMES AND ACTIVITIES TO REINFORCE ALPHABETICAL ORDER

2.   GAMES AND ACTIVITIES TO REINFORCE
          ALPHABETICAL ORDER (CONT.)

3.   GAMES AND ACTIVITIES TO REINFORCE MATCHING
          CAPITAL AND LOWER CASE LETTERS   133

3. GAMES AND ACTIVITIES TO REINFORCE MATCHING
CAPITAL AND LOWER CASE LETTERS (CONT.)

4. GAMES AND ACTIVITIES TO REINFORCE LETTER SOUND
RELATIONSHIPS 167

4. GAMES AND ACTIVITIES TO REINFORCE LETTER SOUND RELATIONSHIPS (CONT.)

Methods for Helping Students Who Have Great Difficulty   227

Commercial Instructional Materials   231

HOW TO USE THESE GAMES MOST EFFECTIVELY

When introducing a letter of the alphabet to your students, begin by using the program that has been selected by your school district. Then select several reinforcing activities from this book to follow up that instruction. The number and types of activities you select will depend upon the ease with which children in the group learn the letter.

If you initially teach a letter to the entire class as a group and provide several reinforcing activities for the entire class, you will find that some of the students have learned the letter well while others require further instruction on that letter. More reinforcement activities should be selected from this book to provide additional help for those students who need further instruction.

Students who have already mastered the letter with the initial instruction should be allowed to do other types of activities while additional instruction is provided for the group needing further instruction.

After many or all of the letters have been introduced and learned, you can select games and activities to maintain the learning that has taken place.

1

GAMES AND ACTIVITIES TO REINFORCE LETTER RECOGNITION, LETTER FORMATION, AND ORAL LETTER SEQUENCE

AN ALPHABET MARCH

PURPOSE: Alphabet oral letter sequence

MATERIALS: None

PREPARATION: None

PROCEDURE: Once or twice a day, perhaps just before lining up for recess, have the students line up and march around the room as they say the alphabet to the rhythm of their marching feet.

SAY: We are going to have an alphabet march. Line up single file. The first person in the line will be our leader. We are going to march around the room. Each time we put a foot down we will say the next letter of the alphabet. When we have finished saying the alphabet, we will choose another person to be the leader and we will march again.
     Ready? A . . . B . . . C . . . D . . .

TACTILE BOX

PURPOSE: Letter recognition and letter formation

MATERIALS: shallow box with a lid
            scissors
            Con-Tact paper
            red, green, or blue construction paper
            rubber cement
            table salt

PREPARATION: Cover a shallow box with Con-Tact paper. Cut a piece of red, green, or blue construction paper to fit the inside of the box. Glue the construction paper to the inside box bottom. Pour table salt into the box to cover the bottom, approximately ½" deep.

PROCEDURE: Have the student practice forming the letter being worked on by tracing the letter in the salt, using his index finger and his middle finger as his "pencil."
     This activity works best with an individual child or a small group of children, so that you can make sure that each child is forming the letter correctly. Make sure that each student is using the fingers on the hand with which he usually writes (his dominant hand).
     If a child forgets how to form the letter, take his fingers in your hand and help him print the letter in the salt one or more times. Provide him with a model to refer to as he prints the letter himself.

SAY: We are going to practice forming the letter (H) in the salt. Hold up your index finger and middle finger. We will use these two fingers as a "pencil." Print the letter (H) in the salt. As you print the letter with your fingers, say the name of the letter softly aloud.

      Shake the box to erase the letter. Now print the letter several more times in the salt, each time pronouncing the letter name softly to yourself.

LETTER OF THE DAY STICKER

PURPOSE: Letter recognition

MATERIALS: a yard of several solid, bright colors of Con-Tact paper
      scissors
      permanent black wide felt-tip marker

PREPARATION: Cut out squares, circles, or seasonal shapes from Con-Tact paper or other similar adhesive-backed plastic cloth. Print the letter being reviewed on the Con-Tact paper.

PROCEDURE: After instruction is provided on the letter name, peel off the paper backing and stick the Con-Tact paper letter sticker on to the child's clothing—a shirt sleeve or pants leg just above the knee—with the letter facing toward the child so that he is not reading it upside down.

      Ask the other children in the room to ask him quietly throughout the day what the name of his letter is. If he cannot remember, the other child can tell him the letter name. By constantly seeing the letter stuck on his clothing and being frequently asked and/or told the letter name throughout the day, the child should have the letter mastered by the time school is over for the day.

      If he has not learned the letter name by the time school is over, when he arrives home from school his parents will see his letter sticker. They will realize that their child is working on learning that letter and it is to be hoped that they will give him more help in learning the letter.

      The letter stickers are excellent to use with:

1. A child who is having great difficulty learning the alphabet and cannot remember a letter from one day to the next.
2. A child who has mastered most of the letters but just can't remember a few of the letters.
3. A group of children who are just learning the letter name after having it introduced for the first time.

SAY: We have been learning the letter (P). To give you more practice in recognizing this letter, I am going to stick a letter sticker on your clothing. Off and on during the day, I want you to look at that letter sticker and think of its letter name. If you forget the letter name, ask someone else whom you think would know or come ask me. You may also want to practice printing the letter on paper.

I am also going to ask the other children in the class to ask you the name of the letter throughout the day. If you forget the letter name, another student will tell you its name.

When you go home after school, show your parents the letter sticker and tell them the letter name.

LETTERS ON HANDS

PURPOSE: Letter recognition

MATERIALS: washable, *non-toxic* felt-tip marker

PREPARATION: None

PROCEDURE: Using a washable, *non-toxic* felt-tip marker, print a newly presented letter on the hand of each child learning the letter. Off and on throughout the day, ask the children to look at their hands and name the letter.

When the children go home, parents seeing the letter on their child's hand will know that this letter is presently being learned. It is to be hoped that the parent will then help the child learn that letter name.

If a parent objects to letters being marked on his or her child's hand, discontinue the procedure with that child. Be sure to use only a washable, *non-toxic* felt-tip marker.

This same procedure can be used with letters that certain children have difficulty learning. Thus, it can be used on an individual as well as a group basis.

SAY: I am going to print the letter we have been learning on the palm of your hand. Look at your hand off and on throughout the day and remember the letter name. If you forget the letter name, ask someone in the class whom you are sure would know or ask me.

Off and on throughout the day I will be asking you to look at your hand and tell me the letter name.

When you go home, tell your parents the letter name. Tell them the letter name again just before you go to bed.

GLUE AND SALT TACTILE ALPHABET CARDS

PURPOSE: Letter recognition and letter formation

MATERIALS: 52 unlined file cards
white school glue
a school-type paintbrush, ½″ wide
blue tempera paint
red tempera paint
2 paper cups
table salt
shoe box
attractive Con-Tact paper

PREPARATION: Here is a simple way to make an excellent set of inexpensive tactile letter cards.

Pour approximately ⅓ cup of white school glue into a paper cup. Stir in enough blue tempera paint to give the glue a pretty, fairly deep blue color. If powdered tempera paint is used, add a small amount of water to the mixture to bring the glue back to normal consistency.

Next, dip the paintbrush into the glue mixture and brush a capital A on the first file card, using a generous amount of glue. Next, sprinkle the glue generously with salt. Set that card off to the side to dry thoroughly. Continue using the same procedure for the capital letters B-Z.

Now mix the red tempera paint with the white glue in another cup. Then use the same procedure for making the lower case letter cards.

Let the cards dry overnight. Shake off the excess salt. File in alphabetical order in a shoe box that has been covered with attractive Con-Tact paper.

PROCEDURE: Select a letter card. Tell the student the name of the letter on the card. Take his index finger and middle finger in your hand and guide his fingers over the letter in the correct way for printing the letter. As you do this, have him say the name of the letter aloud. Have him trace over the letter with his fingers several more times by himself, each time saying the letter name and forming the letter in the correct manner. Then have the child print the letter several times on a sheet of paper using a crayon, saying the letter name each time he prints it.

SAY: Today we are going to learn a new letter and how to print it. On this card is the letter (F). Give me your index finger and middle finger. Let me guide your fingers over the letter in the correct way, while we say the letter name aloud.

Now trace over the letter with your two fingers several more times by yourself. Each time you trace the letter, say the letter name softly to yourself.

Next, print the letter on a sheet of paper using a crayon. Say the letter name each time you print it.

SANDPAPER TACTILE ALPHABET CARDS

PURPOSE: Letter recognition and letter formation

MATERIALS: scissors
sheets of medium coarse sandpaper
2 sheets of bright-colored railroad board or posterboard (2 different colors)
paper cutter
rubber cement
sheet of paper
crayon

PREPARATION: Cut 26 pieces, each 4″ × 4″, from each color of posterboard.
Next, cut the 26 capital letters and the 26 lower case letters out of sandpaper, making the large letters approximately 3″ high. Glue a different sandpaper capital letter onto each of the 26 pieces of posterboard of one color. Glue a different sandpaper lower case letter on each of the 26 pieces of the other color of posterboard.

PROCEDURE: Select a letter card. Tell the student the name of the letter on the card. Take his index finger and his middle finger in your hand and guide his fingers over the letter in the correct way for printing the letter. As you do this, have him say the name of the letter aloud. Have him trace over the letter with his fingers several more times by himself, each time saying the letter name and forming the letter in the correct manner. Then have the child print the letter several times on a sheet of paper using a crayon, saying the letter name each time he prints it.

SAY: Today we are going to learn a new letter and how to print it. On this card is the letter (V). Give me your index finger and middle finger. Let me guide your fingers over the letter in the correct way while we say the letter name aloud.

Now trace over the letter with your two fingers several more times by yourself. Each time you trace the letter, say the letter name softly to yourself.

Next, use a crayon to print the letter on a sheet of paper. Say the letter name each time you print it.

ALPHABET SONG

PURPOSE: Alphabet oral letter sequence

MATERIALS: piano (optional)
                     record with the *Alphabet Song* (optional)
                     record player (optional)

PREPARATION: None

PROCEDURE: Sing the *Alphabet Song* with the children often.

PLAY DOUGH LETTERS

PURPOSE: Letter recognition and letter formation

MATERIALS: commercial or homemade play dough
                     chalk
                     chalkboard

PREPARATION: RECIPE FOR HOMEMADE PLAY DOUGH
                 flour ⎫
                         equal amounts
                 salt ⎭
                 tempera paint
                 water

Knead flour, salt, tempera paint, and water together to reach a play dough consistency and the desired color. Substitute food coloring for tempera paint, if desired. Store in an airtight plastic bag and refrigerate when not in use. This play dough will dry solid when left exposed to air.

Print the letter being learned on the chalkboard. Have a chunk of play dough for each student.

PROCEDURE: Have students make the letter being learned out of play dough. Have the letter printed on the chalkboard or on a card in front of the students. Have the students take a handful of play dough, roll it into a "snake," then bend it around and break pieces off to correctly form the letter. If desired, let the play dough letters dry thoroughly, and then allow the students to take the letters home.

SAY: Who can remember the name of the letter on the chalkboard? Yes, it is the capital letter (M). We started learning the letter (M) yesterday.

I am going to give you each a chunk of play dough. Today we are going to make the letter (M) out of play dough. First, roll your play dough into a long snake, like this . . . (demonstrate). Now, break off pieces of your snake and push them together to form the capital letter (M).

Very good. Now mash your play dough back into a ball, then roll out another snake to make the capital letter (M) again.

Now let's make the lower case (m) out of our play dough.

ALPHA-BIT SORT

PURPOSE: Letter recognition

MATERIALS: alphabet spaghetti or alphabet cereal

PREPARATION: Pour a pile of alphabet spaghetti or alphabet cereal onto the center of a table.

PROCEDURE: Have the student(s) sort out all of the (r's), or whatever letter you specify. Several students could do this at the same time, each one assigned to a different letter to search for and sort out of the pile.

SAY: I have poured a pile of alphabet spaghetti on this table. I want you to sort all of the (r's) out of the pile. Before you begin, go up to the chalkboard and print the capital and lower case (r). Good. Whenever you find a capital or lower case (r), put it here in a separate pile. When you have sorted out all you can find, I will come to see how many you were able to find.

TRACING LETTERS

PURPOSE: Letter recognition and letter formation

MATERIALS: tagboard
                permanent black felt-tip marker
                tracing paper

PREPARATION: Print the alphabet letters on sheets of tagboard, as illustrated.

PROCEDURE: Have the student place a sheet of tracing paper over the letters and trace them. A student can practice printing the letters often, using new sheets of tracing paper as needed.

SAY: Today you are going to practice printing the letters of the alphabet. Here is a set of alphabet cards and here are several sheets of tracing paper.

Before you begin, let's make sure you know all of the letter names. Point to each letter and name it for me.

Now place a sheet of tracing paper over one card. Hold the tracing paper firmly with one hand so that it doesn't slide around. Then trace over each letter with your pencil.

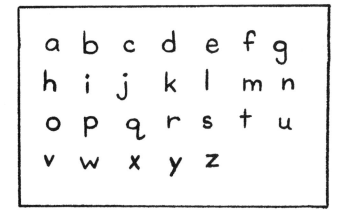

or

PIPE CLEANER LETTERS

PURPOSE: Letter recognition and letter formation

MATERIALS: pipe cleaners
alphabet cards

PREPARATION: None

PROCEDURE: Give each student several pipe cleaners. Let the students form the letters out of pipe cleaners.

After use, most of the pipe cleaners can be smoothed out and used again another day.

SAY: I am going to give each of you several pipe cleaners. Who can tell me the name of the capital and lower case letter on the card I am holding? That's right. It is the letter (d).

Pick up one of your pipe cleaners and bend it, like this (demonstrate), to form the capital letter (D).

Now pick up another pipe cleaner and bend it around to make the lower case letter (d).

TRACE-IT ERASE-IT CHALKBOARD ACTIVITY

PURPOSE: Letter recognition and letter formation

MATERIALS: chalkboard (not black)
washable black felt-tip marker
yardstick
chalk

PREPARATION: This activity works well on any color of chalkboard except a black one. With a washable black felt-tip marker and a yardstick, draw lines on a section of the chalkboard to represent lines on writing paper. Make the lines low enough that the students can easily write on them.

At the left end of the chalkboard, use the washable felt-tip marker to print the letter the children have difficulty remembering or printing correctly. Then print the letter 3 or 4 times in dotted lines.

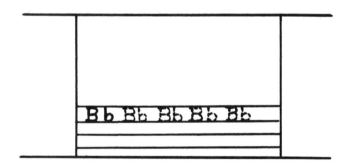

PROCEDURE: Have students who are having difficulty with that letter go to the chalkboard in their spare time and practice writing the letter. Have the students trace over the solid letter and the dotted letters with a piece of chalk. Have them erase their chalk letters and trace them again and again. After tracing and erasing the letters a number of times, they can practice printing the letters on the lines without using the dotted letters. The washable felt-tip marker letters and lines will stay on the chalkboard until washed off with a wet cloth.

Students who have difficulty remembering the name of the letter should be told the name of the letter before they start tracing it. Then they should softly say aloud the name of the letter *each* time they form the letter.

SAY: (Michael), will you come to the chalkboard, please? On the chalkboard I have printed the letter (w). Here is the capital (W) and here is the lower case (w). With your index finger and your middle finger, let's trace over the capital and lower case (w).

Here is a piece of chalk. Trace over the letters with the chalk. As you trace each letter, softly say the name of the letter. Now trace over the dotted letters.

Now let's erase the board and you can trace over the letters again and then again.

After you have traced over the letters a number of times, try printing them as neatly as you can on the lines underneath. Remember, each time you print the letter say the name of the letter softly.

You may come back to the chalkboard and practice the letter (w) whenever you have free time.

TRACE-IT ERASE-IT BLACKBOARD ACTIVITY
FOR BLACK CHALKBOARDS
(A recipe for special non-erase chalk)

PURPOSE: Letter recognition and letter formation

Note: The Trace-It Erase-It Chalkboard Activity previously described can be done on black chalkboards using specially prepared white chalk instead of the washable felt-tip marker.

MATERIALS: 1 cup water
⅓ cup sugar
6 pieces of *soft* white chalk (the kind you buy in toy stores—*not* school chalk)
pan
stove
aluminum foil
jar with lid
blackboard

PREPARATION: Here is a recipe for making a chalk that can be removed from a blackboard by wiping it off with a damp cloth.

Bring the water and sugar to a boil. Remove from heat. Put the chalk into the water and let it soak for 45 minutes. Remove the chalk from the water. Place the chalk on aluminum foil and let it dry overnight. Store in a jar with a lid.

PROCEDURE: With the specially prepared white chalk, and a yardstick, draw lines on a section of the blackboard to represent lines on writing paper. Make the lines low enough so that the students can easily reach to write on them.

At the left end of the blackboard, use the specially prepared chalk to print the letter the children have difficulty remembering or printing correctly. Then print the letter 3 or 4 times in dotted lines.

The students, using regular chalk, trace over your dotted letters. They erase and do it again and again. Your specially treated chalk cannot be erased by the students with an ordinary chalkboard eraser, but will wipe off easily with a damp cloth.

This chalk can be used on chalkboards of various colors, not just on black chalkboards.

This specially treated chalk can also be used to draw lines on the blackboard on which students can practice their printing.

SAY: (Joan), will you come to the blackboard, please? On the blackboard I have printed the letter (H). Here is the capital (H) and here is the lower case (h). With your index finger and your middle finger, let's trace over the capital and lower case (H).

Here is a piece of chalk. Trace over the letters with the chalk. As you trace each letter, softly say the name of the letter. Now trace over the dotted letters.

Now let's erase the board and you can trace over the letters again and then again.

After you have traced over the letters a number of times, try printing them as neatly as you can on the lines underneath. Remember, each time you print the letter, say the name of the letter softly.

You may come back to the chalkboard and practice the letter (H) whenever you have free time.

MAGIC SLATES

PURPOSE: Letter recognition and letter formation

MATERIALS: magic slates (inexpensive discount store variety)

PREPARATION: None

PROCEDURE: Have students practice their printing on magic slates. The magic slates provide a high interest alternative to printing letters on paper.

SAY: We are going to practice printing our new letters on magic slates. The letters are printed on the chalkboard. Who can come to the chalkboard and tell us the names of these letters?

Now print the capital and lower case letter (t) on your magic slates. Pull up the two sheets of plastic film to erase the letters. Then print them again . . . and again.

Practice the other letters in the same way. Each time try to print that letter neater than the one before!

As you write on your magic slates, I will walk around and you can show me how neatly you are forming your letters.

TRANSPARENCY OVERLAY LETTER MATCHING

PURPOSE: Visual perception, matching letters

MATERIALS: 9″ × 12″ sheet of oaktag or railroad board
felt tip marker
permanent black transparency marking pen
heavy transparency film, acetate, or clear heavy plastic
small manila envelope
rubber cement
laminating materials (optional)
scissors
art knife

PREPARATION: Use the felt-tip marker to print various letters of the alphabet on the oaktag or railroad board. Space the letters well apart in uneven rows, as illustrated.

Next, cut out squares of clear plastic. The squares should all be the same size and should be a little larger than the largest letter printed on the card. You will need the same number of plastic squares as you have letters on the card.

Place one plastic square over each letter on the card. Use the permanent black transparency marking pen to print each letter on the plastic film that is on top of it. Be careful to trace exactly over each letter on the card so that each letter on the plastic film matches the letter on the card *exactly*.

Glue a small manila envelope to the back of the card. Laminate the card with the envelope flap open. Carefully slit open the envelope opening. Store the plastic film letters in this envelope when they are not in use.

You may wish to prepare several cards like this using different letters. Students will work on this activity board individually.

PROCEDURE: The students match letters on plastic film squares to identical letters on the activity board.

SAY: On this card are some of the letters of the alphabet. On the back of the card is an envelope. In the envelope are small plastic squares with the same letters printed on them. Carefully take out all the plastic squares. Spread them out. Pick one up and place it on top of the letter on the card that matches it. Line the letter lines so that they fit on top of each other exactly. Continue doing the same with each of the letters.

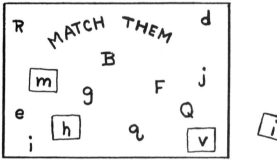

DOTTED LETTERS

PURPOSE: Letter formation

MATERIALS: Sheet of paper
felt-tip marker
pencil or crayon

PREPARATION: With the felt-tip marker, dot the lines of the letter to be worked on on a sheet of paper.

PROCEDURE: Take the child's index finger and middle finger in your hand and guide these fingers over the lines of the letter in proper letter writing sequence. Next, have the child make the lines solid by tracing over the dotted lines with a pencil or crayon. Make sure that the child forms the parts of the letter in the proper manner and in the proper sequence of lines.

SAY: This is the capital letter (E) and here is the lower case letter (e). Give me your index finger and your middle finger. I am going to pretend that your fingers are my pencil. I am going to trace over the capital (E) with your fingers. Now close your eyes and let me trace over the capital (E) again with your fingers.

Open your eyes. Here is a crayon. Trace over the capital (E) with the crayon to make the lines solid.

Let's do the same thing with the lower case (e). Give me your fingers and we will trace over the (e). Now close your eyes and let me use your fingers to trace over the (e) again.

Open your eyes. Here is the crayon. Trace over the lower case (e) with the crayon to make the lines solid.

COVER THE CHALKBOARD!

PURPOSE: Letter recognition and letter formation

MATERIALS: assorted colors of chalk
chalkboard

PREPARATION: None

PROCEDURE: Give the student an assortment of colors of chalk. Select a letter that is giving the student difficulty. Print the capital and lower case forms of the letter on the chalkboard. Tell the student the name of the letter. Holding his hand in yours, guide his hand as he traces over the letter with his fingertips. Have him name the letter as he traces it. Repeat the procedure several times. Rewrite the letter on the chalkboard.

Next, tell the student that he is to cover that section of the chalkboard with the letter using the various colors of chalk, printing the letter in various sizes and at various angles. (See the illustration.) Each time the student prints the letter, he is to say its name softly aloud.

Note: This activity is excellent for the student who has difficulty remembering the letter names from one day to the next.

SAY: (Bobby), I have printed a capital (R) and a lower case (r) on the chalkboard. Give me your index finger and your middle finger on the hand with which you write. I am going to hold your two fingers in my hand and trace over the capital (R) on the chalkboard. As we trace over the letter with your fingers, say (R) softly aloud. Let's trace over it again . . . and again. Say the name of the letter each time. Now you trace over it by yourself while I watch.

Let's do the same with the lower case (r). Give me your fingers again. Let's trace over the (r) . . . again . . . and again. Now trace over it by yourself several times. Say the names of the letter each time.

Here is a box of various colors of chalk. I want you to cover this section of chalkboard with the letter using various colors of chalk, printing the letter in various sizes and at various angles. Each time you print the letter, say the letter name softly aloud.

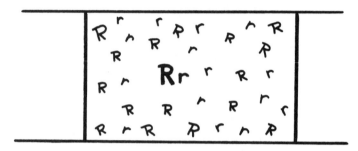

GLUE-A-LETTER

PURPOSE: Letter recognition and letter formation

MATERIALS: bright-colored construction paper, one sheet for each student
white school glue
rice, macaroni, cereal, corn, marshmallows, etc.

PREPARATION: None

PROCEDURE: Have students glue objects onto bright-colored construction paper to form the letter. Examples of things that can be glued on include: rice, macaroni in the shape of wagon wheels, pieces of cereal, miniature marshmallows, corn, beans, etc.

Have the students dribble glue onto the construction paper to form the letter. Then have them put pieces of corn, or whatever material they are using, on the paper to form the lines of the letter. Allow to dry overnight.

For students who have difficulty forming the letters, you may want to print the letter with a pencil on their construction paper before you give them the paper. Then they can dribble the glue on the lines of the letter and finish the project with a minimum of difficulty.

SAY: I am going to give you each a sheet of construction paper. While I am passing out the paper, please get out your bottles of glue. Next, I am going to give you each a handful of corn.

I have printed a capital (C) and a lower case (c) on the chalkboard. Who can name some objects that begin with the sound of (C)? . . . Corn also begins with the sound of (C).

Today we are going to make a capital (C) and a lower case (c) on our paper using corn! First print your name on one side of the paper. Then turn your paper over. Take your bottle of glue and dribble a capital (C) on your paper. Then take pieces of corn and place them in the glue to form the capital (C). (Demonstrate.)

Make a lower case (c) on your paper in the same way.

When you are finished, we will set your papers up to dry. When the glue is completely dry, you may take the papers home to hang in your bedrooms.

TACTILE ALPHABET BOOK

PURPOSE: Letter recognition and letter formation

MATERIALS: 26 sheets of 9″ × 12″ tagboard
assortment of cloth of different types, colors and patterns (cotton, felt, velvet, corduroy, wool, brushed nylon, etc.)
large ring binder notebook
rubber cement
paper punch
scissors
permanent black felt-tip marker

PREPARATION: Cut large alphabet letters out of cloth. Glue a different letter on each sheet of tagboard. Punch 3 holes in the left side of each page and insert into the ring binder notebook. Write Alphabet Book on the front of the notebook.

Variation: A fancier book cover can be made by using a carpet sample (available free or at a nominal cost at stores selling carpets) and 3 large size notebook rings (available at office supply stores). Fold the carpet sample in half. Insert the pages and mark on the carpet sample where holes will need to be punched. Take out pages. Punch the holes with an ice pick or other suitable device. Put notebook rings through one side of the carpet. Insert the pages, putting the rings through the holes in the pages. Push the rings on through the holes on the back part of the carpet book cover. Then snap the rings shut.

PROCEDURE: Let students look at the Tactile Alphabet Book often, feeling the letters and tracing over the letters with their fingers.

SAY: Boys and girls, I want to show you a very special alphabet book I made especially for you. Each page has a different letter on it. The letters are made out of cloth and are meant for touching, feeling, and tracing over with your fingers.

Look! Aren't the letters beautiful? Some are soft and fuzzy. Some are smooth. And some are rough and bumpy.

The letters are in A-B-C order. You can start at the beginning of the book tracing over the letter A with your fingers, like this . . . (demonstrate). Then turn the page, think the letter name, then trace over that letter with your fingers. Continue on through the alphabet book in this way. If you forget a letter name, ask someone you are sure would know.

You will want to "read" this special alphabet book many many times.

LAMINATED PRINTING PRACTICE CARDS (I)

PURPOSE: Letter formation

MATERIALS: assorted colors of construction paper
fine felt-tip marker
washable black felt-tip marker
ruler
laminating materials or clear Con-Tact paper
grease pencils, china marking pencils, or washable transparency
marking pens
paper towels

PREPARATION: On each sheet of construction paper draw lines with the fine felt-tip marker. The lines should be spaced approximately like those on first grade writing paper.

On the left side of each paper print the capital or lower case form of the various letters, one letter beneath the other, using the washable felt-tip marker. Laminate or cover with clear Con-Tact paper.

You will also need grease pencils or washable transparency marking pens.

PROCEDURE: Have the students practice printing each of the letters on the laminated practice cards, using grease pencils, china marking pencils, or washable transparency marking pens.

SAY: I have a set of cards that will help you learn to print the letters of the alphabet better and better. These are called Printing Practice Cards. Here are the special marking pencils you use to print on these cards.

To use these, choose a card and get one of the special marking pencils. Look at the letter printed on the first set of lines. Then, using your special pencil, neatly and carefully print that letter again and again on that line. Then look at the letter printed on the next set of lines. Neatly and carefully print it several more times on that line.

When you have finished practicing your printing on that card, get a tissue or a paper towel and carefully wipe off your letters. Then place the card and the special marking pencil back on the shelf ready for another student to use. You may work on a Printing Practice Card whenever you have time.

LAMINATED PRINTING PRACTICE CARDS (II)

PURPOSE: Letter formation

MATERIALS: first grade writing paper
sheets of tagboard
scissors
rubber cement
laminating materials or clear Con-Tact paper
fine felt-tip marker
grease pencils, china marking pencils, or washable transparency
marking pens
paper towels

PREPARATION: Cut the tagboard and the writing paper to the same size. Glue one sheet of writing paper onto one side of each sheet of tagboard.

On the left side of each sheet of writing paper, print a capital or lower case form of the various letters, one letter beneath the other. Laminate or cover with clear Con-Tact paper.

You will also need grease pencils or washable transparency marking pens.

PROCEDURE: To use, have the students practice printing each of the letters on the laminated practice cards, using grease pencils, china marking pencils, or washable transparency marking pens. When finished, the students wipe off their writing with tissue or paper towels. The practice cards can be used again and again.

SAY: I have a set of cards that will help you learn to print the letters of the alphabet better and better. These are called Printing Practice Cards. There are the special marking pencils you use to print on these cards.

To use these, choose a card and get one of the special marking pencils. Look at the letter printed on the first set of lines. Then, using your special pencil, neatly and carefully print that letter again and again on the next set of lines. Neatly and carefully print it several more times on that line.

When you have finished practicing your printing on that card, get a paper towel and carefully wipe off your letters. Then place the card and the special marking pencil back on the shelf ready for another student to use. You may work on a Printing Practice Card whenever you have time.

SURPRISE BOX

PURPOSE: To provide skill maintaining practice in any area

MATERIALS: a large square box with a lid
scissors
tape
colored paper
2 different colors of paper or construction paper
rubber cement
miscellaneous copies of duplicator exercises

PREPARATION: Cut a circle out of the box lid, approximately 5″ in diameter. Tape the lid to the box. Cover the box with paper of a solid attractive color. Leave the hole exposed.

Out of a contrasting color of construction paper or kraft paper, cut out the letters for the words Surprise Box. Glue these letters onto one side of the box to form the 2 words. Out of another attractive color of construction paper, cut out a number of question marks. Glue these here and there on the box.

Variation: If you want to be fancier about the opening to the box, cut a circle about 7″ in diameter from an old inner tube. Cut slits in the inner tube center. Staple the inner tube to the inside of the box lid so that it covers the hole in the lid, as illustrated. Put book binding tape over any sharp ends of staples so that no child can get scratched.

The student can easily reach his arm through this opening and pull out a paper. But he cannot see into the opening.

Whenever you run off duplicator exercises on letter recognition, letter formation, alphabetical order, letter-sound relationships, etc., run off a number of extra copies. Fold each extra copy into quarters and place in the Surprise Box. When the surprise box is well-stocked with miscellaneous exercises, stir well, then introduce it to the class. Continue adding duplicator pages to the box daily.

PROCEDURE: When students finish other work early, let them reach into the Surprise Box and pull out a duplicator exercise to do.

SAY: Look! Today we are going to begin using a Surprise Box! It contains surprise practice papers for us to do—lots and lots of different kinds of practice papers!

Whenever you finish your work, come to the box, reach your arm in, feel around and pull out a surprise exercise. If it is too difficult an exercise for you, or, if it is the same one that you have drawn out of this box before, fold it up, put it back in, and pick another. Then take it back to your seat and do it. When you have finished it, make sure your name is on it, then put it on my desk. You may do as many papers from the Surprise Box as you possibly can!

FINGER PAINT FUN!

PURPOSE: Letter recognition and letter formation

MATERIALS: finger paints
finger paint paper or shelf paper, one sheet for each student
water

PREPARATION: None

PROCEDURE: Have students print the letter being worked on in finger paint, smooth it over and print it again.

When it is time to quit, have the student make the letter one last time making it "the neatest you have ever made it." Allow to dry. Then let the student take it home.

SAY: We have been learning the letter (D). Today we are going to finger paint the capital and lower case (D).

I am going to give each of you a sheet of paper. I want you to go to the sink one at a time and wet the paper on both sides. Then take your paper to your place at the table and smooth it out flat on the table with the shiny side up. Then I will come around with the bottle of finger paint and put a blob of finger paint on your paper.

Now smear the finger paint over the surface of the paper with the palm of your hand. Then print a capital (D) and a lower case (d) in the paint using your index finger and middle finger as your "pencil." Smooth the paint over by rubbing the palm of your hand gently over the paper. Then form the letter (D) again and again in the same way. If your paint begins to dry too much, raise your hand and I will come add a few drops of water to your paint.

APPLE CARDS

PURPOSE: Manuscript letter formation

MATERIALS: red railroad board
light green railroad board
scissors
black medium felt-tip marker
laminating materials or clear Con-Tact paper
2 washable transparency marking pens or china marking pencils
2 small boxes, decorated
paper towels

PREPARATION: Cut 26 apples from red railroad board and 26 apples from light green railroad board. Draw stems on one side of each apple.

Using the felt-tip marker, print with dashes a different capital letter on each red apple. Print with dashes a different lower case letter on each green apple. (See the illustration.)

Laminate the apples or cover with clear Con-Tact paper.

Decorate 2 small boxes. Put the red apples in one box and the green apples in the other box. Put a china marking pencil or a washable transparency marking pen in each box.

PROCEDURE: Have the students practice printing the letters, tracing over the letters on the laminated Apple Cards using china marking pencils or washable transparency marking pens. Students wipe off the cards and use them again and again.

SAY: We have been making nice progress on learning to print the capital and lower case letters of the alphabet. Today we have some fancy new cards to help us improve our printing even more. These cards are called Apple Cards. The red apple cards are for practicing the capital letters. The green apple cards are for practicing the lower case letters.

     In each box there is a set of apples and a special marking pen. Take out an apple and carefully trace over the lines of the letter using the special marking pen. Never use a regular pencil. Always use the special pencil. As you mark over the lines of the letter, think the letter name to yourself. If you have forgotten the letter name, ask a friend whom you are certain would know the letter.

     Do each apple card in your box as neatly and carefully as you can. Then get a paper towel and carefully wipe off your marks on each apple card. Put the cards and the special marker back into the box and put the box on our activity table ready for another student to use.

     You may do the other box another day. You will want to practice your printing on these cards many days.

ALPHABET BOOKS

PURPOSE: Oral letter sequence and letter recognition

MATERIALS: a variety of good alphabet books from the library or bookstore

PREPARATION: None

PROCEDURE: There are numerous good alphabet books on the market. These can be read to the class occasionally. These books should also be set out so that the children can take them to their seats and "read" them often. And do allow the students to sign them out to take home for their parents to read aloud to them.

PEGBOARD LETTER LACING CARDS

PURPOSE: Letter recognition

MATERIALS: pegboard
high gloss paint (optional)
paintbrush (optional)
permanent black felt-tip marker
long boot laces
saw

PREPARATION: Saw 26 pieces of pegboard, approximately 8″ × 10″. If unpainted, paint one side with a high gloss paint. Using the felt-tip marker, print the letters of the alphabet so that the letter lines go over the holes in the pegboard, one letter to each piece of pegboard. The capital letters should be approximately 8″ high and the lower case letters should be approximately 4″ high. You will also need a number of long boot laces.

Variation: Instead of cutting 26 pieces of pegboard, cut 2–6 pieces. Print selected letters on the boards with a *washable* felt-tip marker. When students are ready for new letters, wash off the letters, dry the surface thoroughly, then print on new letters with washable felt-tip marker.

PROCEDURE: Have the student tell the name of the letter, then lace the letter with the boot lace by going in and out of the holes on the pegboard along the letter lines. Encourage the student to lace the letter lines in the correct sequence.

SAY: I have a set of letter lacing boards that I am going to place on the activity table. You may get one to lace whenever you have time.

When you get one, bring it up and tell me the name of the letter on that board. Then take it to your seat along with one of the laces. Lace the letter with the lace by going in and out of the holes on the board along the letter lines.

When you have finished the letter, put it on my desk for me to see. Then I will unlace it and put it back on the activity table ready to be done again.

SEW A LETTER

PURPOSE: Letter recognition and letter formation

MATERIALS: Styrofoam packaging trays, one for each student
yarn
yarn needles
scissors
permanent felt-tip marker

PREPARATION: You will need Styrofoam packaging trays, the kind in which meat and fruits are packaged in grocery stores. You will need one for each student in the group. You may want to ask each child to bring one from home. You will also need yarn and a number of yarn needles.

Select a letter that is being learned by the group. On each Styrofoam tray dot in the lines of that letter. Cut pieces of yarn longer than the length needed to sew around the letter lines. Thread yarn into needles and knot one end of each piece of yarn.

PROCEDURE: Have students sew around the outline of the letter. Since the children are working with needles, this activity needs constant teacher supervision and should be done with only a small group at a time.

Variation: The children can sew the capital form of the letter on one tray and the lower case form of the letter on another tray using another color of yarn.

SAY: I am going to print our new letter on the chalkboard. What letter is this? . . . Yes, it is the letter (F). We were learning this letter (yesterday). We are going to sew our new letter today!

First I am going to hand each of you a Styrofoam tray with our letter dotted on it. Next, I am going to give each of you a needle threaded with yarn. Be careful with the needle! It is sharp.

Now watch how I am going to sew my letter. (Demonstrate.) See how I make the needle go in and out along the lines of the letter (F). You may begin to sew your own letter (F) now. If you have difficulty I will help you. When you have finished sewing the letter (F), give it to me. I will take off the needle and knot the end of the yarn. You may take your letter (F) home with you to show Mommy and Daddy.

CUT OUT AND GLUE LETTERS

PURPOSE: Letter recognition and letter formation

MATERIALS: duplicator master
duplicator paper
duplicator machine
scissors
bottles of white school glue
bright-colored construction paper, one sheet for each student
crayons

PREPARATION: On a duplicator master, print the outline of the selected capital and lower case letter, so that the letter may be colored in later. Run the master off onto sheets of white duplicator paper.

You will also need a sheet of bright-colored construction paper for each student, and scissors, white school glue and crayons for each student.

PROCEDURE: Give each child a letter paper and a sheet of bright-colored construction paper. Have the children carefully cut out the letter, then glue it onto the construction paper.

SAY: Yesterday we learned a new letter. (Print the letter on the chalkboard.) It looked like this. Who can remember the name of this letter? . . . That's right! It is the letter (H). And who can tell us a word that begins with the sound of the letter (H)? . . . Good!

Now I am going to give you each a sheet of paper with the capital (H) and lower case (h) printed on it. While I pass these out, get out your scissors, crayons, and glue. Next, I am going to give you each a sheet of construction paper.

Put the paper with the capital and lower case (H) in front of you. Place your finger on the capital (H). Trace over the capital (H) on your paper like this. (Demonstrate.)

Now color the capital (H) and the lower case (h) with your crayons. Next, with your scissors carefully cut out the capital (H) and glue it on your construction paper. Then cut out the lower case (h) and glue it on to the construction paper.

When you have finished, your paper should look like this. (Hold up a sample completed paper.)

LETTER SEARCH POSTER

PURPOSE: Letter recognition

MATERIALS: old magazines and newspapers
construction paper, one sheet for each student
scissors
white school glue

PREPARATION: None

PROCEDURE: Give the students some old magazines and newspapers. Have them cut out a specified letter each time they find it. Have the students paste the letters on a piece of construction paper to make an attractive poster. This can be an individual activity or a group activity.

SAY: On the chalkboard I have printed a capital (N) and a lower case (n).

I have placed a stack of magazines and newspapers and a stack of construction paper on the table. I want you to get one magazine or newspaper and one sheet of construction paper and take it to your desk. Look through the pages of the magazine or newspaper and cut out each capital (N) or lower case (n) that you can find. Then paste the letters onto a piece of construction paper to make a pretty poster.

When you have finished your poster, it will probably look something like this. (Hold up a sample completed poster.)

PRINT IT IN CLAY

PURPOSE: Letter recognition and letter formation

MATERIALS: Plasticine clay or play dough
heavy paper, one sheet for each student
pencils

PREPARATION: None

PROCEDURE: Give each student a blob of Plasticine clay or of play dough. And give each student a fairly large piece of heavy paper on which to work with his or her clay.

Have the students mash their clay flat and smooth. Print the letter to be practiced on the chalkboard and call on a student to tell its name. Then have the students print the letter in the clay with their pencil points by pushing the pencil point into the clay and "dragging" the pencil through the clay to form the letter. Provide help for any student having difficulty.

Have the students smooth over the surface of the clay and print the letter again and again, each time softly saying the name of the letter.

Note: Do make sure that the students hold their pencils in a correct writing position during this activity. And do make sure that the students are forming the letter lines in the correct sequence and manner.

SAY: On the chalkboard I have printed a capital (R) and a lower case (r).

Today we are going to practice printing in clay. I am going to give you each a blob of clay and a sheet of heavy paper on which you are to work with your clay.

I want you to mash your clay flat and smooth. (Demonstrate.) Then I want you to print a capital (R) in the clay with your pencils. Push your pencil point right into the clay and drag it through the clay to print the letter (R) deep in the clay.

Then smooth the clay over and print the lower case (r) in it. Print the letters over and over again in this way. Each time you print the letter, softly say the name of the letter.

INSTRUCTIONAL CASSETTE TAPE

PURPOSE: Alphabet letter sequence and letter recognition

MATERIALS: cassette tape
cassette tape recorder
earphones
alphabet book

PREPARATION: Prepare your own instructional tape for a cassette recorder. You might begin the tape by singing the *Alphabet Song,* then asking the listening student to sing the *Alphabet Song* along with you.

Next, select a good alphabet book and read it into the tape with pauses between pages. The student will look at the alphabet book while listening to this part of the tape.

Next, you might slowly say the alphabet and then repeat it, asking the student to say it with you.

Add other alphabet instructional songs or activities, depending upon the instructional needs and skill level of the students.

PROCEDURE: Put the cassette player with a set of earphones and the alphabet book in a convenient place to make an alphabet listening center.

SAY: Children, I have set up an alphabet listening center here. There is an instructional tape in the cassette tape player and a set of earphones plugged into it.

You may come up one at a time, put on the earphones, turn on the tape player, and listen. Do what the tape tells you to do. When the tape tells you to sing the *Alphabet Song,* softly sing the *Alphabet Song.* When the tape tells you to pick up the alphabet book beside the tape player and follow along in the book, do so.

When you have finished listening to the tape, rewind the tape by pushing this button. Then go back to your seat. Another student may then come up and listen to the tape. You may listen to the tape more than one time if you wish.

If you have forgotten how to use the tape player, ask (designate a student) to show you.

FEEL, HANDLE, AND TAKE HOME LETTERS

PURPOSE: Letter recognition and letter formation

MATERIALS: Styrofoam packaging trays, 2 trays for each student
scissors
permanent felt-tip marker

PREPARATION: You will need Styrofoam packaging trays of the kind in which meat and fruits are packaged in grocery stores. You will need 2 trays for each student in the group.

Select the letter that is being learned by the group. Using a pair of good scissors, cut the capital and lower case form of that letter out of the Styrofoam trays. Cut the capital letter as large as possible. Cut the lower case letter in the correct proportion to the capital letter. Put a tiny dot on the bottom front side of each letter. This will allow the students to determine if they have the letter right side up.

PROCEDURE: Distribute a capital and lower case form of the letter to each child after having provided initial instruction on the letter. The students can feel the letter, handle the letter, etc. Then they can take the letter home to play with it and become more familiar with the letter.

SAY: (On the day you introduce the new letter to the class, provide instruction in the manner you determine. *Then* give each child his own Styrofoam letters.)

Now I am going to give you each a Styrofoam capital and lower case letter (F). Turn the letters so that the tiny dots are at the bottom of the letters. Take the capital letter (F) and with your fingers trace over it. Now close your eyes and feel all over it. What is the name of the letter? . . . Now hold the lower case letter (f). Make sure that you are holding the letter so that you can see the dot at the bottom of the letter. Use your fingers to trace over the letter. What is the name of the letter? . . . Now close your eyes and feel the letter.

You may take your capital and lower case letter (F) home with you today. Handle them carefully because they will break. Show Mommy and Daddy your letters and tell them the letter name. Play with the letters. Practice tracing over the letters with your fingers. Then put them in a place in your bedroom where you can see them easily. When you wake up tomorrow, look at those letters and think of the letter name. If you forget the name, ask one of your parents. When you come in the classroom tomorrow, come whisper the letter name to me.

WORD SEARCH POSTER

PURPOSE: Letter recognition

MATERIALS: chalkboard and chalk
old magazines, catalogs, workbooks
white school glue
scissors
colored construction paper, posterboard or railroad board

PREPARATION: None

PROCEDURE: Select a letter. Print the capital and lower case form on the chalkboard. Talk about the name of the letter.

Have the students search through old magazines, catalogs, and workbooks to find words that begin with that letter. They do not need to know what the word says—this activity is strictly for letter recognition. Have them cut out words that begin with that letter and glue them onto colored construction paper, posterboard or railroad board.

This can be an individual activity with each child making his own word search poster, or it can be a group activity with every child in the group finding words to glue onto one large poster.

SAY: I have placed a pile of magazines, catalogs, and old workbooks on this table. I have also set several large sheets of colored posterboard here.

I am going to divide the class into groups with three students in a group. Each group should get a piece of posterboard and several magazines, workbooks, or catalogs. Then find an area in which your group would like to work.

Search through your magazines, etc., to find words that begin with the letter (p). Every time you find a word that begins with that letter, cut it out and glue it on your posterboard. You don't need to know what the word says, it just has to begin with the letter (p).

The group with the most words on their poster at the end of (20) minutes will be the Word Search Poster Champions!

BLINDMAN LETTER SEARCH

PURPOSE: Letter recognition

MATERIALS: plastic letters or alphabet blocks
blindfold

PREPARATION: Spread plastic letters or alphabet blocks on a table.

PROCEDURE: Blindfold a student. Name a letter. Have the student locate the letter by touch only.

SAY: I have spread a set of plastic letters on the table. I am going to put a blindfold on (Billy). Then I will name a letter. (Billy) will feel around in the letters to find the letter I named.

It will then be (Judy's) turn to be blindfolded and search for the next letter I name.

FEEL IT LETTER SEARCH

PURPOSE: Letter recognition

MATERIALS: plastic letters or alphabet blocks with raised letters
blindfold
letter cards

PREPARATION: None

PROCEDURE: Spread plastic letters or alphabet blocks on a table. Show the student a card with a letter printed on it. Blindfold the student. Mix up the letters on the table. Have the student locate the letter by touch only. Continue using the same procedure with other letters.

Use this activity with a small group or an individual student.

SAY: I have spread a set of plastic letters on the table. I am going to show you a letter card. Then I am going to put a blindfold over your eyes and let you find that letter in the pile of plastic letters by feeling each letter until you find the correct letter.

FEEL IT LETTER SEARCH GAME

PURPOSE: Letter recognition

MATERIALS: plastic or wooden letters
blindfolds
letter cards

PREPARATION: None

PROCEDURE: Spread two or three sets of plastic or wooden letters on a table. Show two or three students a card with a letter printed on it. Blindfold the students. Mix up the letters on the table. Have the students race to find the letter by touch only. The first student to find the letter wins. Continue the game using the same procedure with other letters.

SAY: I have spread three sets of plastic letters on the table. I am going to show
        the three of you a letter card. Then I am going to blindfold all three of
        you. I'll mix up the plastic letters on the table. When I say "Go," feel
        each letter until you find the one shown on the card. The first one to find
        that letter will be the winner. We will play this game several times using a
        different letter each time.

CANNED ALPHABET FUN

PURPOSE: Letter recognition

MATERIALS: empty can with a plastic snap-on lid (e.g. a can in which nuts are
                    packaged)
              bright solid-colored Con-Tact paper
              scissors
              permanent felt-tip marker
              railroad board or construction paper
              rubber cement
              paper fastener
              paper clip
              spoon

PREPARATION: Paint the can or cover it with bright solid-colored Con-Tact
        paper. Print Canned Alphabet Fun on the side of the can.
            To make the lid into a spinner, cut out a circle of railroad board or
        construction paper to fit neatly on top of the plastic lid. Draw lines to
        divide the circle into 3 equal pie-shaped sections. Write the numeral 1 in
        one section of the circle, 2 in another, and 3 in another. Glue the circle
        onto the top of the plastic lid. Put a paper fastener through a paper clip,
        then insert the paper fastener through the center of the circle and lid. Bend
        the prongs of the paper fastener so that the paper clip can spin easily. (See
        the illustration.)
            Now cut pieces of railroad board into small circles (or squares). You
        will need enough to fill the can at least halfway. Print a different letter on
        each circle, some capital letters and some lower case letters. Place the
        letters in the can.
            You will also need a spoon.

PROCEDURE: Two to four players play the game. Players take turns spinning
        the spinner and scooping out spoonfuls of letters and naming the letters.
        Each player must name each of the letters he spooned out. He must put
        back into the can each letter that he cannot name. It is then the next
        player's turn to spin the spinner, scoop out letters, and name them.

SAY: We have a new game that 2, 3, or 4 of you may play at a time. The game is called Canned Alphabet Fun.

     To play, the first player spins the spinner. If the spinner lands on the number 2, the player puts the spoon into the can and scoops out 2 spoonfuls of letters. He must then name each of the letters he spooned out. He must put back into the can each letter that he cannot name. It is then the next player's turn to spin the spinner, scoop out letters, and name them.

     When each player has had (6) turns, the player with the most letters is the winner.

SQUIRREL AND ACORNS

PURPOSE: Letter recognition

MATERIALS: 1 large cutout of a squirrel (teacher-made or commercial)
               masking tape
               26 acorn cutouts (teacher-made or commercial)
               washable black felt-tip marker
               laminating equipment or clear Con-Tact paper (optional)

PREPARATION: A cutout of a squirrel can be bought at bookstores in the fall or through school supply catalogs any time of the year. (Instead of purchasing a squirrel cutout, you can make your own on oaktag, railroad board or posterboard. If your artistic ability is lacking, find a picture of a squirrel, put it under an opaque projector, trace it on to your cardboard, then color it appropriately.)

     Next, make 26 acorns out of oaktag. The acorns should each be the same size. Color them appropriately. On one side of each acorn print a different letter of the alphabet.

     Laminate the squirrel and acorns or cover them with clear Con-Tact paper.

PROCEDURE: Tape the squirrel on the chalkboard. Place the letter acorns on a table, letter side down or letter side up. Have students in the group, one at a time, select an acorn and name the letter on that acorn. If the student correctly identifies the letter, stick a loop of masking tape (sticky side out) to the back of the acorn, and have the student "feed it to the squirrel" by sticking it on the chalkboard near the squirrel. If he cannot identify the letter, he must put the acorn down and wait for another turn. Students take turns "feeding the squirrel" until all the acorns are used.

SAY: Here is a very hungry squirrel. Would you like to feed him? On the table are some acorns. Acorns are his favorite food.

Let's take turns feeding him acorns. (Johnny), come up and pick up an acorn. If you can tell us the letter printed on that acorn, I will put a piece of tape on that acorn and you can stick it up on the chalkboard near the' squirrel. If you cannot name the letter on the acorn you can't feed it to our squirrel. You will have to put it back on the pile of acorns on the table.

CATCH A BUTTERFLY
(A bulletin board activity)

PURPOSE: Letter recognition

MATERIALS: assorted colors of construction paper
scissors
washable black felt-tip marker
push pins
bulletin board

PREPARATION: Cut out 26 butterflies from various colors of construction paper as illustrated. (If you wish to use both upper and lower case letters in this activity, then cut out 52 butterflies. Print a different letter of the alphabet on each butterfly.

Using push pins (small bulletin board pins with colorful plastic spool-shaped heads), pin the butterflies onto a bulletin board with the letter side turned toward the bulletin board. The butterflies should be pinned on in a random letter order.

PROCEDURE: The students will take turns unpinning butterflies. As each student unpins a butterfly, he/she must turn it over and identify the letter printed on the butterfly. If able to correctly identify the letter, the student has "caught" that butterfly and may keep it. If unable to correctly identify the letter, the student must pin that butterfly back on the bulletin board.

This activity should be used with an instructional group of from two to six students.

SAY: On the bulletin board are a number of butterflies. We shall see how good you are at "catching" butterflies. When it is your turn, walk up to the bulletin board, unpin a butterfly, put the pin in the box I am holding, then turn the butterfly over and name the letter on the butterfly. If you can name the letter correctly, you have "caught" that butterfly. If you cannot name the letter correctly, you must pin the butterfly back on the bulletin board. It will then be the next student's turn to "catch" a butterfly.

You may keep all of the butterflies you catch. You may take them home and use them to decorate your room if you wish.

CATCH A BEANBAG

PURPOSE: Letter recognition (optional: letter sound relationships)

MATERIALS: assorted solid colors of cloth
scissors
felt
sewing machine
beans

PREPARATION: Make 4 beanbags out of various *solid* colors of cloth. Cut material into eight 5″ squares. Select 8 letters that have already been taught to the class, but which need review work to reinforce or maintain recognition skills. Cut the selected letters out of felt. With a sewing machine, sew one letter on each cloth square. Sew pairs of cloth squares together on three sides, fill partially full of beans, then sew up the fourth side.

PROCEDURE: Have students stand in a large circle. Hold up the beanbags, one at a time, and have the students name the letters. Provide some additional instruction if necessary.

Then toss a beanbag to one of the students. The student will try to catch the beanbag and name the letter facing up on the beanbag. The student will then throw the beanbag back to the teacher. The teacher will throw the beanbag to another student, continuing the game in this manner.

This activity is appropriate for a group of 4–8 students.

Note: Students could be required to name the letter and name an object that begins with that letter.

SAY: Let's stand up and form a large circle. In my hands I have 4 beanbags. On each beanbag are 2 different letters, one on one side and another on the other side. Let's make sure that you remember the names of each of these letters. (Hold up the beanbags, one at a time, and have the students name the letters.)

We are going to play a game with these beanbags. I am going to toss a beanbag to one of you. The person to whom the beanbag is tossed will try to catch it. He will then name the letter on the beanbag. The letter to be named will be the one that is facing up in that person's hand. He will throw the beanbag back to me. I will throw the same or a different beanbag to someone else. We will continue the beanbag game in this manner.

LETTER RECOGNITION TACHIST-O-SCOPES

PURPOSE: Letter recognition

MATERIALS: colored railroad board or lightweight posterboard
scissors
tagboard or heavy art paper
pencil
felt-tip marker
paper cutter
art knife

PREPARATION: Cut out a seasonal shape, an animal shape, or any other interest-catching shape from the railroad board or posterboard. (See the illustration.) Make the shape 8″–12″ high. In approximately the middle of the cutout object, cut 2 horizontal slits approximately 3″ long, ¼″ wide, and 2″ apart. Next, cut strips 2″ wide from tagboard or heavy art paper. With a pencil, lightly mark 2″ intervals on the strips. Use the felt-tip marker to print a letter in each of the spaces on these strips.

      Put one of the letter strips behind the cutout object, thread it through the bottom slit, then back through the top slit.

PROCEDURE: To use, the teacher slides the letter strip up exposing one letter. The student(s) names the letter. Then the teacher pulls the letter strip to expose the next letter, etc.

SAY: I have a (friendly whale) who wants to help you review the letters of the alphabet. When I slide a letter into the window on the (whale), name that letter.

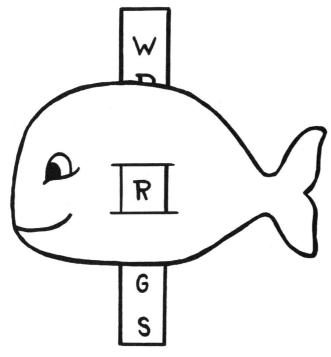

DRAW IT–NAME IT

PURPOSE: Letter recognition

MATERIALS: compass
             yellow construction paper or yellow railroad board
             washable black felt-tip marker
             scissors
             laminating materials (optional)

PREPARATION: Using a compass, draw 26 circles on yellow construction paper or on yellow railroad board. Cut out the circles. Outline the circles on one side with a washable black felt-tip marker. On that same side draw smiling faces on each of the circles.

   Turn the circles over. Print a different letter of the alphabet on each of the circles. Laminate if possible.

PROCEDURE: Spread out the smiling face cards on the table with the smiling faces up. Have the students take turns drawing cards and naming the letters on the cards.

SAY: We are going to play a game of Draw It—Name It. We will spread out all of the smiling face cards on the table with the smiling faces up. Then we will take turns drawing the cards and naming the letters on the cards.

GRANDFATHER CLOCK

PURPOSE: Letter recognition assessment

MATERIALS: 16" × 22" sheet of colored railroad board
             felt-tip marker
             paper punch
             yarn
             scissors
             bookbinding tape or masking tape
             2 buttons

PREPARATION: Draw a picture of a grandfather clock on the colored railroad
    board. Print each of the capital letters in a random order going up one side
    of the clock. Print each of the lower case letters in a random order going
    up the other side of the clock.

    Punch a hole at the top and bottom of each side of the clock. Cut 2
    lengths of yarn. Put one end of each piece of yarn through the holes at the
    bottom of the clock. Knot each piece of yarn on the back side of the
    cardboard. Put a piece of bookbinding tape or masking tape over each
    knot. Turn the cardboard back over. String a large button onto each piece

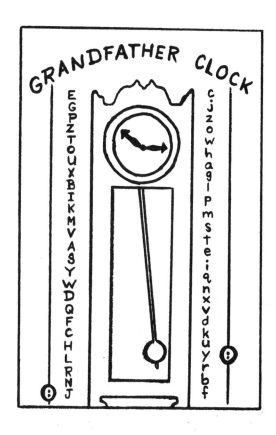

of yarn. Then insert the remaining end of each piece of yarn through the holes at the top of the clock. Knot and tape the yarn on the back of the cardboard.

PROCEDURE: The Grandfather Clock should be used by the teacher with one or two students at a time. The clock can be used to test the students' letter recognition skills. The teacher notes on a piece of paper exactly which letters each student did not know or was unsure of. The teacher later provides instruction on those letters for those individual students needing further instruction.

SAY: Let's see how well you can recognize the letters of the alphabet. This is Grandfather Clock. Slide both of the buttons to the bottom of the clock. Start with the button on the right. Move the button up beside the first letter and name that letter. Then slide the button up beside the next letter and say its name. Continue moving up the clock in this manner, naming each letter. Then do the same on the other side of the clock.

THE MAGIC HAT GAME

PURPOSE: Letter recognition and letter formation

MATERIALS: construction paper
colored pencils
felt-tip markers
scissors
man's hat
cotton
glue
chalk
chalkboard

PREPARATION: Cut 26 rabbits, each approximately 3 " long, out of construction paper. Color in rabbit features with the pencils. Glue a small piece of white cotton on each rabbit tail. Print a different capital letter on each rabbit. Put the rabbits in a man's hat.

PROCEDURE: Have the students take turns pulling rabbits out of the hat, identifying the letter printed on the rabbit, and printing the letter on the chalkboard.

SAY: Children, have you ever seen a magician pull a rabbit out of a hat? Today you will each get to pull a rabbit out of this hat. When you pull the rabbit out of the hat, please tell us what capital letter is printed on your rabbit.

Then go to the chalkboard and print the capital letter and then the lower case letter. When you have finished, return to your chair. It will then be another student's turn to pull a rabbit out of the hat, name the letter, and go to the chalkboard to print the letter.

ALPHABET BINGO

PURPOSE: Letter recognition

MATERIALS: tagboard
                   paper cutter
                   felt-tip markers
                   scissors
                   small pictures cut from catalogs or workbooks
                   rubber cement
                   unlined file cards
                   construction paper
                   laminating materials (optional)

PREPARATION: Make bingo cards out of tagboard using the format illustrated. On each card print a letter in each box (omitting the center square), but vary the letters and the order of the letters on each card.

     Cut out cute little pictures from catalogs or workbooks and glue a different one in the center square of each card.

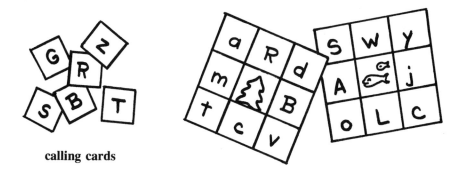

calling cards

     Next, cut 26 file cards in half and print a different capital or lower case letter on each card. These will be the "calling cards."

     Finally, cut up construction paper to make squares for the students to use to cover the letters as they are called.

PROCEDURE: Shuffle the calling cards and lay them face down in a pile. Draw the top card and name the letter on it. The students look at their cards to see if they have the letter. If they have the letter they cover it with a marker. Continue calling letters in this way. The winner is the first player to cover three letters in a row.

SAY: We are going to play Alphabet Bingo. I will give you each an Alphabet Bingo card and 9 construction paper markers.

Place one construction paper marker on the center square. Next, I will shuffle the calling cards and lay them face down in a pile. Now I will draw the top card and name the letter on it. The card says (capital F). Look at your cards to see if you have that letter. If you have the letter (capital F), cover it with a construction paper marker. Now I will pick up the next calling card and name the letter on it. If that letter is on your bingo card, cover it with a marker. We will continue playing in this manner until someone has covered 3 letters in a row, either up and down, or from one side to the other, or from corner to corner. That player then calls BINGO, and we will stop playing. He or she will read aloud the letters covered in his winning line. I will check my used calling cards to make sure I called the letters he has covered. If he has covered them correctly, he wins the game.

We will play the game several times so you will have several chances to win.

CANDY STORE

PURPOSE: Letter recognition

MATERIALS: brown construction paper or brown railroad board
white colored pencil or white chalk
white felt-tip marker (optional)
laminating materials (optional)
small paper bags, one for each student
paper cutter

PREPARATION: Cut 26 or 52 chocolate bar-sized rectangles from brown construction paper or brown railroad board. These will be the ''candy bars.'' Color the ends of each candy bar white with white colored pencil or chalk. Print a different capital and/or lower case letter in the center of each candy bar with the white felt-tip marker. (See the illustration.) Use white colored pencil or chalk if the white marker is unavailable. Laminate, if desired.

You will also need a small paper bag for each child in the group.

PROCEDURE: Spread out the candy bars, letter side down. Give each student in the group a small paper bag. Have the students take turns picking up candy bars, identifying the letters on the candy bars, and placing candy bars in their bags.

SAY: Today we are going to play Candy Store. I am going to put a lot of candy bars on the table. Each candy bar has a different letter printed on it. I am going to put the candy bars letter side down. Then I am going to give you each a paper sack for your candy.

You will take turns picking up candy bars. When you pick up a candy bar, name the letter on the candy bar, then you can put the candy bar in your paper bag. If you cannot name the letter correctly, you must put the candy bar back in the pile. It will then be the next student's turn to pick a candy bar. We will take turns picking candy bars until there are no more left. Then we will count the candy bars to see how many each person got at our candy store.

*BROKEN LETTERS**

PURPOSE: Letter recognition, letter formation, letter-sound relationships

MATERIALS: oaktag or railroad board
felt-tip marker
pictures cut from old workbooks, catalogs, etc.
rubber cement
paper cutter
laminating materials or clear Con-Tact paper
manila envelope or box, 4″ × 4″ or larger

PREPARATION: Cut 26 squares, each 3″ × 3″, from oaktag or railroad board. Print a different capital letter on each card. On the back of each card glue a picture of an object that begins with the sound of that letter. Glue the picture right in the center of the card.

---

*Indicates a self-correcting activity.

Next, cut each card either horizontally or vertically through the center of the card. The cut should be a straight cut that passes through the letter on one side and the picture on the other side. Laminate all pieces or cover with clear Con-Tact paper. Keep the pieces in a box or manila envelope when not in use.

Variation: You could make a set of lower case letter cards using the same procedure. Be sure to make the letter cards a different color and store them in a separate container.

PROCEDURE: Have the students find and fit together the two halves that form each letter. This activity is self-correcting. If the students fit 2 halves together to form a letter correctly, the card when flipped over will show a picture of an object that begins with the sound of that letter.

Note: For young children, children having difficulty, or children with short attention spans, you may want to limit the number of letter cards in the activity.

SAY: Children, in this box is a new activity that I am going to place on our activity shelves. When you have some spare time, you may select this new activity to do.

In this box you will find capital letter cards. There is one letter card for each letter of the alphabet. However, each letter card has been cut in half from top to bottom or from one side to the other side. You will need to find the 2 pieces that belong together and put them together to form the capital letter. When you think you have put a letter together correctly, turn the card over. You will see a picture of an object that begins with the sound of that letter. (Demonstrate.) If you have put the wrong parts together, the picture won't look right and you will know that you need to look again to find the correct letter parts.

When you have finished one letter card, go right on and do the rest. You will want to work on this activity by yourself or with one friend.

STOP! THAT'S NOT RIGHT!

PURPOSE: Letter recognition and/or assessment of student learning

MATERIALS: set of capital and lower case letter cards
oaktag cards, 2 for each student
green felt-tip marker
red felt-tip marker
compass

PREPARATION: You will need a set of cards with a different capital or lower case letter printed on each card. You will also need 2 signal cards for each student in the group. One signal card for each student should have a large green circle on one side. The other signal card for each student should have a large red circle on it.

PROCEDURE: Hold up a letter card and say a letter name. If the letter name you said is the right one for the letter on the card, the students hold up their green circle signal cards. If the letter you said is not the correct one for the letter on the card, the students hold up the red circle signal card.

SAY: When a car comes to a stop light what does a red light mean? . . . Yes, it means *Stop*. What does a green light mean? . . . Yes, it means *Go*.

I am going to give you each a signal card with a red circle and a signal card with a green circle. When I hold up a letter, I will say a letter name. If the letter name is the right one for the letter on the card, hold up your green circle signal card. The green circle means, "Go on, that letter is correct."

If the letter I say is *not* the correct one for the letter on the card, hold up the red circle signal card. The red circle means, "Stop! That's not right!"

ERASE THE BOARD

PURPOSE: Letter recognition and alphabetical order

MATERIALS: chalkboard
chalkboard eraser
assorted colors of chalk

PREPARATION: Print some or all capital and lower case letters on a section of the chalkboard, using various colors of chalk, and printing the letters in a random order and slanted at different angles. (See the illustration.)

PROCEDURE: Students take turns going to the chalkboard and erasing the letters on the chalkboard in alphabetical order.

Variation: Have the students take turns going to the chalkboard and erasing the letters as you name them in random order.

SAY: We are going to take turns going up and erasing the letters on the chalkboard in alphabetical order. The first student will erase the capital and lower case A. The next student will erase the capital and lower case B, etc., until the board is entirely erased.

ALPHABET PRESENTS

PURPOSE: Letter recognition

MATERIALS: unlined file cards or sheets of oaktag
paper cutter
washable felt-tip markers and/or colored pencils
laminating materials (optional)
chalkboard
chalk

PREPARATION: Cut unlined file cards or sheets of oaktag into varying sizes and shapes of presents. You will need 52 in all. On one side of each, draw ribbons and bows with washable felt-tip markers or colored pencils. (See the illustration.) On the other side print a capital or lower case letter, a different letter on each present. Laminate, if possible.

PROCEDURE: Place all presents, ribbon side up, on the table. Students take turns choosing presents and naming the letters on the presents. If a student cannot name the letter, he should be told the name of the letter and be, asked to print the letter on the chalkboard several times as he repeats its name.

SAY: Everyone enjoys presents. Look what we have on our table—lots of beautiful presents!
    We are going to take turns picking presents. When you pick a present, tell us the name of the letter on the other side, then place the present on the table beside you. It will then be the next student's turn to choose a present.

If you do not know the letter on the present you choose, we will tell you the name of the letter. Then you can print that letter on the chalkboard several times.

BEANBAG THROW

PURPOSE: Letter recognition

MATERIALS: chalkboard
chalk
beanbag

PREPARATION: Select 5–10 or more letters that you want the group to drill or review. Divide one section of the chalkboard into that number of parts. Print a different letter in each area, as illustrated. You will also need a beanbag.

PROCEDURE: Have the students line up and take turns throwing a beanbag at the chalkboard. When a student hits a section of the chalkboard he must name the letter in the section the beanbag hits. It is then the next student's turn.

This activity works best with a group of 2–8 students.

Variation: Students can be required to name the letter, then name a word that begins with the letter. Students hitting the same letter should be expected to think up words not previously named.

SAY: I have divided this section of the chalkboard into a number of parts. Each part has a letter printed in it. We are going to line up and take turns throwing a beanbag at the chalkboard. The first person will throw the beanbag. Then he must name the letter in the section the beanbag hits. It is then the next person's turn. You will each have several turns. If the beanbag hits right on a line between 2 letters, the player will have to tell us the name of both letters.

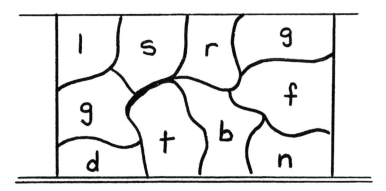

LEARN AND PRACTICE LETTER TEDDY BEARS

PURPOSE: Letter recognition

MATERIALS: construction paper, tagboard, or railroad board
scissors
washable fine felt-tip markers
laminating materials or clear Con-Tact paper
notebook ring(s)
paper punch

PREPARATION: Cut 26 teddy bears out of one or more colors of construction paper, tagboard, or railroad board. Fill in the features on both sides of the teddy bears using *washable* fine felt-tip markers. Print a different letter of the alphabet on each teddy bear, printing the capital letter on one side and the lower case letter on the reverse side. (See the illustration.)

Laminate or cover with clear Con-Tact paper, then punch a hole in each teddy bear.

Finally, you will need a notebook ring (available from school and office supply stores).

PROCEDURE: After 6 or more letters have been taught, put the teddy bears with the letters already taught on the notebook ring. Put the ring of letter teddy bears out for the students to pick up and practice naming the letters. Occasionally, take the teddy bears off the ring and use them as flashcards to review the letter names with the group. Then place them back on the ring. As each new letter is taught to the group, add that letter teddy bear to the ring.

Variation: You may want to make a set of letter teddy bears for each child in the group having difficulty learning the letter names. As each new letter is presented, the corresponding letter teddy bears can be added to each child's own letter teddy bear ring. Each child could be allowed to take his ring of letter teddy bears home to keep as soon as he has learned to correctly name each of the 26 letters.

SAY: On this ring is a set of teddy bears. Each teddy bear has a letter printed on him. You will find each of the letters we have learned so far on these teddy bears. I will put the letter teddy bears on the activity table. When you have free time, get the ring of letter teddy bears and review the letters on them. If you forget a letter name, ask someone you are certain would know. Sometimes you may want to say the letter names with a friend.

    As we learn new letters, I will add teddy bears with those letters to the ring. Practice the letter teddy bears often.

STUDENT ALPHABET BOOKS

PURPOSE: Letter recognition and letter formation

MATERIALS: sheets of 9″ × 12″ unlined white paper
                      sheets of 12″ × 18″ colorful construction paper, one for each
                              student
                      paper fasteners or stapler and staples
                      felt-tip marker
                      crayons

PREPARATION: You will need one sheet of 12″ × 18″ colorful construction
           paper for each student.
                      Fold the sheets of construction paper in half. These will be the
           covers for the alphabet books. With a felt-tip marker, print the words
           Alphabet Book and a child's name on the front cover. Do the same with
           each of the other covers, printing a different child's name on each cover.

PROCEDURE: As you present each letter to the class over a period of time,
           have them print the capital and lower case form of the letter many times
           on a sheet of unlined paper. The letter can be printed with different colors
           of crayons and in various arrangements or designs.
                      As each child finishes his letter sheet, put it inside the Alphabet
           Book cover. Any duplicator sheets or other types of activity sheets on that
           letter could also be added to the Alphabet Book.
                      When all of the letters have been completed and put in the Alphabet
           Book, the pages should be put in alphabetical order. The books can then
           be stapled together or secured with paper fasteners.
                      When the Alphabet Books are completed, the children may take
           them home to keep and to share with their parents.

RULER OF THE KINGDOM

PURPOSE: Letter recognition

MATERIALS: 52 unlined file cards
                      felt-tip marker

PREPARATION: Print a different capital or lower case letter on each of 52
           unlined file cards. This will be a set of flashcards.

PROCEDURE: Have the students place their chairs in a straight line, one beside
           the other. Students sit in the chairs with the teacher in front of the students
           facing toward the students. The student sitting in the first chair is sitting in
           the Ruler of the Kingdom chair.
                      The teacher shows the first alphabet card to the student in the Ruler
           of the Kingdom chair. If he can name the letter correctly, he can stay in

his seat. If he cannot name the letter correctly, he must move to the last seat and each player moves up one seat. It is then the next student's turn to name the letter on the next flashcard. Play continues in this way, with each player trying to reach the Ruler of the Kingdom chair and stay there by not missing the flashcard when it is his turn.

The game is over when a predetermined time limit has elapsed or when the flashcards have been gone through a predetermined number of times. The *winner* is the player in the Ruler of the Kingdom chair when the game ends.

Enforce two very important rules in this game:

1. Any player who whispers or says aloud an answer when it is not his turn must go to the end of the line.
2. The first letter name a player says for a flashcard is the one that counts. He cannot say a letter and then quickly change his mind and say another letter.

This game is an excellent means of review and reinforcement of letters already taught. It works well with a small reading group of approximately 3–8 students.

SAY: Children, we are going to play a new game today. It is called Ruler of the Kingdom.

Place your chairs in a straight line, one beside the other. Now sit down on your chairs. I will sit in front of you facing toward you. The player sitting in the first chair in the line is sitting in the Ruler of the Kingdom chair.

I will shuffle the alphabet flashcards. Then I will show the first flashcard to the student in the Ruler of the Kingdom chair. If he can name the letter correctly, he can stay in his seat. If he cannot name the letter correctly, he must move to the last seat and each player moves up one seat. It is then the next player's turn to name the letter on the next flashcard. We will continue playing in this way, with each player trying to reach the Ruler of the Kingdom chair and stay there by not missing the flash card when it is his turn. The *winner* is the player in the Ruler of the Kingdom chair when the game ends.

There are two very important rules in this game:

1. Any player who whispers or says aloud an answer when it is not his turn must go to the end of the line.
2. The first letter name a player says for a flashcard is the one that counts. You cannot say a letter and then quickly change your mind and say another letter.

FAST AND SNAPPY ALPHABET CONDUCTOR GAME

PURPOSE: Letter recognition

MATERIALS: a set of alphabet flashcards (capital and lower case)

PREPARATION: None

PROCEDURE: Students place their chairs in a straight line, one behind another. All students sit except one who stands behind the chair of the first seated player. The student who is standing is the Conductor. The teacher flashes the first letter flashcard. The Conductor and the first seated player race to see who can be the first to name the letter correctly. If the Conductor names the letter correctly first, he moves behind the next player. If the seated player names the letter correctly first, he becomes the Conductor and stands behind the next player while the former sits down in the seat just emptied.

The object is to become the Conductor and stay the Conductor. If desired, the student who is the ''conductor'' at the end of the game can be called the *winner*.

SAY: We are going to review the letters of the alphabet by playing a game called Fast and Snappy Alphabet Conductor.

Place your chairs in a straight line, one behind the other. (Debbie) will start out as our Conductor. She won't put her chair in line. Everyone sits down except (Debbie). You are the passengers in the train and (Debbie) is the Conductor on the train.

The Conductor stands behind the first seated player. I will show a letter flashcard. If the Conductor names the letter correctly first, he moves behind the next player. If the seated player names the letter correctly first, he becomes the Conductor and stands behind the next player while the former conductor sits down in the seat just emptied. The game continues in this way. The object of the game is to become the Conductor and stay the Conductor.

TICKET OUT

PURPOSE: Letter recognition

MATERIALS: a set of alphabet flashcards (capital and lower case)
          washable *non-toxic* felt-tip marker

PREPARATION: None

PROCEDURE: When the students are ready to leave the room for recess, lunch period, or to go home, you can play this game. Have the students sit or line up ready to leave the room. Before they can leave the room, they must each give you a Ticket Out. The Ticket Out is the name of the letter on the flashcard you show the student. As soon as the first student correctly names the letter on the flashcard, he may leave. It is then the next student's turn to name the letter on the next flash card.

When a student cannot correctly name the letter, tell him the name of the letter. Then give him the flashcard and send him to the end of the line to wait his turn again. When it is his turn again, have him tell you the name of the same letter he has on the flashcard that he took to the end of the line. Have him give back the flashcard. Then print that same letter on the palm of his hand with a washable *non-toxic* felt-tip marker.

If the student still cannot remember the letter name, simply tell him the letter name, print the letter on his hand and let him go out of the room.

Note: If not all of the letters have yet been taught, only those flashcards containing letters that have already been taught should be used.

SAY: Please line up at the door. To leave the room you are going to have to give me a Ticket Out. The Ticket Out is the name of the letter on the flash card I show you when your turn comes. As soon as the first student correctly names the letter on the flashcard, he may leave. It is then the next student's turn to name the letter on the next flashcard. If you cannot correctly name the letter, I will tell you the name of the letter. Then you must go to the end of the line and wait your turn again. When it is your turn again, you will tell me the name of the letter you missed the first time.

DUPLICATOR MASTER ALPHABET
ACTIVITY CARDS

PURPOSE: Letter recognition, letter formation, matching capital with lower case letters and/or simple letter sequence

MATERIALS: sheets of 9″ × 12″ tagboard
duplicator masters of the alphabet
duplicator machine
laminating materials or clear Con-Tact paper
washable transparency marking pens, grease pencils, plastic
marking crayons, or china marking pencils

PREPARATION: Select good duplicator masters of the alphabet. Using a duplicator machine, run off one copy of each duplicator master onto the sheets of tagboard. These will be the Alphabet Activity Cards. Laminate or cover the activity cards with clear Con-Tact paper.

You will also need washable transparency marking pens or china marking pencils.

PROCEDURE: Have students practice alphabet skills, marking on the laminated alphabet activity cards with washable transparency marking pens or grease pencils. When a student has completed an alphabet activity card, he should wipe it off so that it is ready for the next student to use.

SAY: Here is a set of alphabet activity cards you may work on when you have finished your other work. You will need to use one of these special marking pens to mark on these cards. (Give special directions on how to do the activity cards in the set.)

SPIN AN ELEPHANT

PURPOSE: Letter recognition

MATERIALS: 18″ × 20″ sheet of colored railroad board
gray or pale blue railroad board
felt-tip markers
compass
scissors
paper fastener
paper punch
laminating materials

PREPARATION: Draw a large circle on the railroad board. Print the letters of the alphabet in a random order around the inside of the circle, as illustrated. Cut an elephant-shaped spinner out of gray or pale blue railroad board. Laminate both pieces. With a paper punch, punch a hole in the center of the elephant spinner. With the point of a pair of scissors, punch a hole in the center of the circle. Insert a paper fastener through the hole in the elephant, then on through the hole in the circle. Bend the prongs of the paper fastener on the back of the cardboard, leaving the paper fastener loose enough so that the elephant spinner will spin easily.

PROCEDURE: The students take turns spinning the elephant spinner and naming the letter to which the elephant's trunk points.

This activity works best with a small group.

SAY: We have a new game called Spin the Elephant. To play the game we will lay the game board flat on the table. Then we will take turns spinning the elephant spinner and naming the letter to which the elephant's trunk points.

RACE TO THE CASTLE

PURPOSE: Letter recognition

MATERIALS: railroad board
assorted colors of wide and fine felt-tip markers
colored pencils
laminating materials or clear Con-Tact paper
spinner
game markers

PREPARATION: On a piece of railroad board, draw and color a game board as illustrated. Laminate or cover with clear Con-Tact paper.
You will also need a spinner and markers.

PROCEDURE: This game can be played by 2–4 players at a time. The players take turns spinning the spinner and moving their markers. Each player must name each of the letters he has moved his marker over as well as the letter on which he landed. The winner is the first player to reach the castle.

Any player unable to name a letter should be told the letter name. He does not lose his turn or have to move his marker back a space for not knowing a letter.

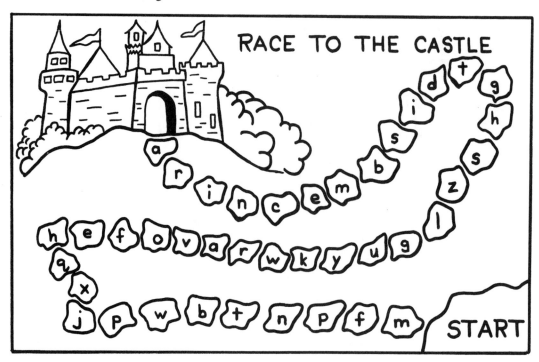

SAY: All players place their markers on *Start*. The first player spins the spinner and moves his marker forward that number of spaces. He must name each of the letters over which he has moved his marker as well as the letter on which he landed. It is then the next player's turn to spin the spinner and move his marker. The *winner* is the first player to reach the castle.

HICKORY DICKORY DOCK

PURPOSE: Letter recognition

MATERIALS: 14″ × 22″ sheet of railroad board
felt-tip markers
game markers
die
laminating materials (optional)

PREPARATION: Draw a picture of a grandfather clock on the sheet of railroad
board. Draw a mouse starting to climb up the left side of the clock. Print
letters up one side, across the top, and down the other side of the clock, as
illustrated. Laminate, if possible.

You will also need game markers and a die.

PROCEDURE: The players take turns throwing the die and moving their markers forward the number of spaces indicated. Each player must name each
of the letters over which he moved his marker, as well as the letter on
which he landed. If a player is unable to name a letter, he must move his
marker back one space. The *winner* is the first "mouse" to reach WIN.

SAY: Here is a game that 2 or 3 of you will enjoy playing together. It is called
Hickory Dickory Dock. The object of the game is to be the first mouse up
the side, across the top, and down the other side of the clock.

Here are the markers. Pretend that each marker is a mouse. Place
your markers on *Start*. The first player throws the die and moves his
marker forward that number of spaces. He must then name each of the
letters over which he moved his marker and the letter on which he landed.

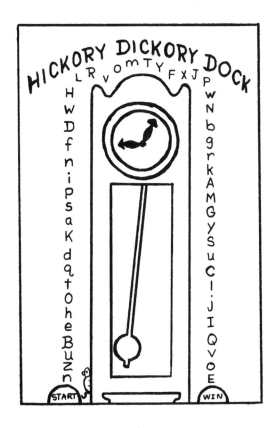

If he is unable to name a letter, he must move his marker back one space. It is then the next player's turn to throw the die and move his marker forward, etc. The WINNER is the first ''mouse'' to reach WIN.

THE THREE BEARS ALPHABET GAME

PURPOSE: Letter recognition

MATERIALS: 14″ × 22″ sheet of colored railroad board
assorted colors of felt-tip markers
colored pencils
game markers
die

PREPARATION: Draw and color a game board on the railroad board, as illustrated. You will also need a die and game markers.

PROCEDURE: The players place their markers on the bears' house. The players take turns throwing the die and moving their markers forward that number of spaces. Each player must name the letter on each of the spaces over which he moved his marker as well as the space on which his marker landed. The *winner* is the first player to return to the bears' house.

Any player unable to name a letter should be told the name of the letter. However, he will not lose a turn or have to move back for not knowing the letter name.

Note: In this game or any board game of this type, be sure that at least 1 of the players thoroughly knows all of the letters and can correct errors. You want to be sure that correct responses are being given as the game is played.

SAY: This game is played by 2–5 players. The object of the game is to be the first player to return to the bears' house. The players place their markers on the bears' house. The first player throws the die and moves his marker forward that number of spaces. He must name the letter on each of the spaces over which he moved his marker and the space on which his marker landed. It is then the next player's turn to throw the die and move his marker. The *winner* is the first player to return to the bears' house.

JUMP IN THE LAKE!

PURPOSE: Letter recognition

MATERIALS: colored railroad board or posterboard
assorted colors of felt-tip markers
scissors
die
game markers
laminating materials or clear Con-Tact paper

PREPARATION: Cut a game board, shaped as illustrated, out of the colored railroad board or posterboard. Draw spaces and waves and print *Start, Win,* and *Jump in the Lake!* Choose 5–26 letters to be used on the game board. Print the selected letters in the spaces around the game board. Laminate or cover with clear Con-Tact paper. You will also need a die and markers.

PROCEDURE: Have the players place their markers on *Start.* The players take turns throwing the die and moving their markers forward the number of spaces indicated by the die. Each player must correctly name the letter on the space on which he landed. If a player is unable to name the letter correctly, his marker must "jump in the lake." He must move his marker into the lake right next to the space on which he landed and he must miss his next turn. When it is his turn again he moves his marker back onto the space he was on before he "jumped into the lake." Then he throws the die and moves his marker forward.

The winner is the first player to reach WIN.

SAY: Today we have a new alphabet game you will enjoy playing. It is called Jump in the Lake! Two to four people may play this game at a time.

The players select their markers and place them on *Start.* The first player throws the die and moves his marker forward that number of spaces. He must then correctly name the letter on the space on which he landed. It is then the next player's turn to throw the die and move. If a player cannot name the letter correctly, his marker must "jump in the lake." He must move his marker into the lake right next to the space on which he landed and he must miss his next turn. When it is finally his turn again, he moves his marker back onto the space he was on before he "jumped in the lake." He then throws the die and moves his marker forward. Play continues in this way.

WIN

PURPOSE: Letter recognition

MATERIALS: 16″ × 22″ piece of solid-colored oilcloth or vinyl
assorted colors of permanent felt-tip markers
game markers
die

PREPARATION: Draw a colorful game board on the oilcloth or vinyl, as illustrated. You will also need a die and game markers.

This game board can be rolled up or folded for easy storage.

PROCEDURE: The players place their markers on *Start* and take turns throwing the die, moving their markers forward the number of spaces indicated, and naming the letters on the spaces over which they moved their markers.

Note: Make sure that at least one of the players knows the letter names thoroughly so that that student can correct any errors the other players make. The teacher must make sure that the students playing the game are not giving incorrect answers and continuing on without being corrected!

SAY: Here is a new game called Win. Two, three, or four people can play this game at a time. Each player will select a marker. The players will place their markers on *Start*. The first player throws the die and moves his marker forward that number of spaces. He must then name the letters on each of the spaces over which he moved his marker and the letter on which he landed. It is then the next player's turn to throw the die and move his marker forward. The winner is the first player to reach *Win*.

   If a player is unable to correctly name one or more letters during his turn, he must move his marker back the number of spaces equal to the number of mistakes. The player *must* be told the correct letter name for each mistake.

RAILROAD RACE

PURPOSE: Letter recognition

MATERIALS: 14″ × 22″ piece of yellow railroad board
permanent felt-tip marker
colored pencils
yardstick

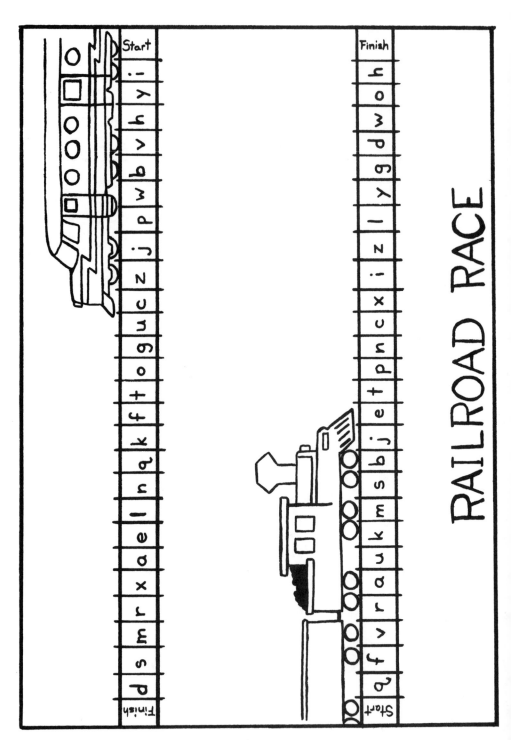

RAILROAD RACE

        sponge
        scissors
        laminating materials or clear Con-Tact paper
        2 game markers

PREPARATION: On the railroad board, draw a game board as illustrated. Color the trains with colored pencils. Laminate the game board or cover it with clear Con-Tact paper.

        To make a die, cut a cube-shaped piece from a sponge. Use the permanent felt-tip marker to write one numeral on each side of the cube, using the numerals 1–3. You will also need 2 game markers.

PROCEDURE: Two players play at a time. Each player chooses a train track and places his marker on the *Start* position. The players take turns throwing the die and moving their markers forward that number of spaces. A player must name each of the letters over which he moveed his marker as well as the letter on which he landed.

        Any player unable to name a letter should be told the name of the letter. He does not lose his turn or have to move his marker back spaces for not knowing the letter name.

SAY: This game can be played by two players at a time. Eac player chooses a train track and places his marker on the *Start* position. The first player throws the die and moves his marker forward that number of spaces. He must name each of the letters over which he moved his marker as well as the letter on which he landed. It is then the next player's turn to throw the die and move his marker along his train track. The *winner* is the first player to reach *Finish*.

THE BUG

PURPOSE: Letter recognition and letter formation

MATERIALS: colored railroad board or posterboard
             permanent felt-tip marker
             scissors
             die
             game markers
             pencil
             several sheets of writing paper
             laminating materials or clear Con-Tact paper

PREPARATION: Out of colored railroad board or posterboard, cut out a game
board as illustrated. Write Start, Win, and The Bug on the game board.
Select 5–26 letters on which you wish the students to drill. Print those
letters in the spaces around the game board. Laminate the game board or
cover with clear Con-Tact paper.

You will also need a die, markers, a pencil, and several sheets of
writing paper.

PROCEDURE: Players take turns throwing the die and moving their markers
forward the number of spaces indicated. A player must correctly name the
letter on the space on which he landed and he must print the letter neatly
on a piece of paper.

Any player who is unable to name the letter on the space on which he
landed or is unable to print the letter, should be told the letter name and/or
shown how to print the letter. He must then move his marker back one
space.

SAY: Today I have a new game you will really enjoy. It is called THE BUG!
How many of you have seen a car that looks something like this?

Now listen carefully while I explain how to play our new game. Not
more than 4 people can play this game at a time. Each player chooses his
marker. The players place their markers on *Start*. The first player throws
the die and moves his marker forward that number of spaces. He must
then correctly name the letter on the space on which he landed. He must
also print the letter neatly on a piece of paper. It is then the next player's
turn to throw the die and move his marker.

Any player who is unable to correctly name the letter on the space on
which he landed or is unable to print the letter, must be told the letter

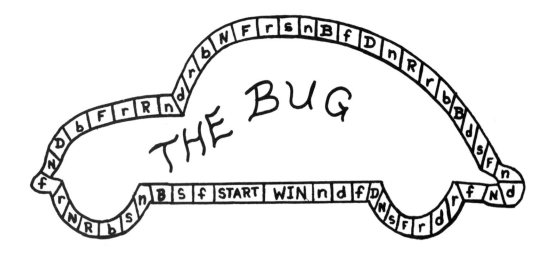

name and/or must be shown how to print the letter. He must then move his marker back one space.

The *winner* is the first player to reach *Win*.

FLOWER POWER

PURPOSE: Letter recognition

MATERIALS: colored railroad board or posterboard
felt-tip markers
scissors
laminating materials or clear Con-Tact paper
yellow construction paper
rubber cement
die
game markers

PREPARATION: Cut a large flower shape out of colored railroad board or posterboard as illustrated. Draw a 1″ border around the flower and mark it off into sections. Print *Start* and *Win* in spaces. Then print selected capital and/or lower case letters in the sections.

Cut a flower center from yellow construction paper. Print the game

name on the flower center. Then glue the center onto the game board. Laminate the game board or cover with clear Con-Tact paper.

You will also need a die and game markers.

PROCEDURE: Students take turns throwing the die, moving forward the number of spaces indicated and naming the letter on the space on which they land.

Variation: Students could be asked to give the letter name and the name of a word that begins with that letter.

Note: The teacher should either supervise the playing of this game or make sure that one of the players definitely and thoroughly knows all of the letters. Otherwise, the students playing the game could give the wrong letter names.

SAY: Children, here is a new game you will enjoy playing. It will help you practice your letter names. Two to four children may play the game at a time.

To play the game, place your markers on *Start*. The first player throws the die and moves his marker that number of spaces. He must then name the letter on the space on which he landed. It is then the next player's turn to throw the die and move his marker forward. Any player who is unable to correctly name the letter on the space on which he landed, must move his marker back 2 spaces. The *winner* is the first player to move his marker onto *Win*. However, to move his marker onto *Win*, the player must throw the exact number needed.

HUNGRY SQUIRREL ALPHABET GAME

PURPOSE: Letter recognition

MATERIALS: colored railroad board or posterboard
permanent felt-tip markers
laminating materials or clear Con-Tact paper
sponge
scissors
game markers

PREPARATION: On a piece of railroad board or posterboard, draw a gameboard as illustrated. Laminate or cover with clear Con-Tact paper.

To make a die, cut a cube-shaped piece from a sponge. Write one numeral on each side of the cube, using the numerals 1–3.

You will also need game markers.

HUNGRY SQUIRREL ALPHABET GAME

PROCEDURE: Players place their markers on the squirrel and take turns throwing the die, moving their markers forward the number of spaces indicated, and naming the letters over which they moved their markers as well as the letter on the space on which they landed.

SAY: This game can be played by 2–4 players at a time. All players place their markers on the squirrel. The first player throws the die and moves his marker forward that number of spaces. He must name each of the letters over which he moved his marker as well as the letter on which he landed. It is then the next player's turn to throw the die and move his marker. The *winner* is the first player to reach the end of the acorn trail and land on the oak leaves.

Any player unable to name a letter will be told the letter name. He does not lose his turn or have to move his marker back a space for not knowing the letter name.

ALPHABET EASTER EGGS
(A student take home and keep game)

PURPOSE: Letter recognition

MATERIALS: large plastic eggs, one for each student
duplicator masters
duplicator machine
sheets of colored construction paper
sheets of heavy white art paper
assorted colors of watercolor felt-tip markers
colored pencils
scissors
masking tape (optional)

PREPARATION: You will need a large plastic egg, the kind that comes apart in the middle, for each student. Each child could be asked to bring one of these eggs to school.

On duplicator masters, draw 26 eggs, all the same size and shape. Each egg when cut out should be as large as can fit easily into the plastic egg. Draw various decorative Easter egg markings on the eggs. Print a different letter of the alphabet on each.

Now run the masters on the duplicator machine onto heavy white art paper and colored construction paper. Run off enough sets of the 26 eggs to give one set to each student in the group plus one extra to keep in the classroom.

Ask parent volunteers or older student volunteers (perhaps sixth graders) to cut out the sets of eggs and to decorate them colorfully with colored pencils and watercolor felt-tip markers.

Put a complete set of decorated alphabet eggs in each plastic egg.

Note: You may want to tape the plastic eggs shut with pieces of masking tape so the children can get them home without losing any of the letter eggs.

PROCEDURE: Near Easter, give each student a set of Alphabet Easter Eggs to take home and keep.

SAY: Today I have something *very* special for each of you! I am going to give each one of you a set of ALPHABET EASTER EGGS. The Alphabet Easter Eggs are going to be your very own! You can take them home with you this afternoon and keep them forever!

I am going to give each of you an egg now. Please don't open the eggs until I have passed them all out. Now open your eggs like this . . . (demonstrate). Inside you will find 26 beautiful Easter eggs. On each egg there is a letter of the alphabet. That makes these eggs extra special because they can help you learn your alphabet letters.

When you take these home, have Mommy and Daddy sit down with you and you tell them the names of the letters you know. Have them help you learn the ones you don't know. Take your eggs out often and practice them.

SAMMY SNAKE

PURPOSE: Letter recognition

MATERIALS: 14″ × 22″ sheet of colored railroad board
kraft paper or wallpaper sample
rubber cement
colored construction paper
felt-tip markers
laminating materials or clear Con-Tact paper
scissors
paper fastener
paper clip
game markers.

PREPARATION: Cut out a snake, as illustrated, from kraft paper or from a wallpaper sample. Glue it onto the railroad board. Divide the snake's body into 26 sections and add his other features. Place a different letter, in random order, in each of the 26 sections of his body. Cut a circle out of colored construction paper. Glue it onto the game board. Divide the circle into 3 or 4 pie-shaped sections. Write a numeral in each section. Laminate the game board or cover it with clear Con-Tact paper.

Punch a hole through the center of the circle. Insert a paper fastener through a paper clip, then through the hole in the circle on the game board. Bend the prongs of the paper fastener, leaving it somewhat loose so that the paper clip will spin easily.

You will also need game markers.

PROCEDURE: Players take turns spinning the spinner, moving their markers forward the number of spaces indicated, and naming the letters on each of the spaces over which they moved their markers and the letter on the space on which their markers landed.

SAY: Two or three players may play this game at a time. Players place their game markers on the snake's tail. The first player spins the spinner and moves his marker forward that number of spaces. He must name the letter on each of the spaces over which his marker moved and the space on which his marker landed. It is then the next player's turn to spin the spinner and move his marker. The *winner* is the first player to reach the snake's head.

Any player who is unable to name a letter will be told the name of the letter. However, the player does not lose a turn or have to move back for not knowing the letter name.

2

GAMES AND ACTIVITIES TO REINFORCE ALPHABETICAL ORDER

HIDE AND FIND LETTER GAME

PURPOSE: Letter recognition and alphabetical order

MATERIALS: thirteen 3″ × 5″ file cards
washable black felt-tip marker
scissors

PREPARATION: Cut thirteen 3″ × 5″ file cards in half. Print a different letter
of the alphabet on each card. Hide the letters around the room.

PROCEDURE: Have the child or children search for the letter cards and identify
the letters on them or put them in alphabetical order.

SAY: Children, we are going to have a Hide and Find Letter Game. I have
hidden letter cards around the room. I want you to search for the cards.
Each time you find a letter card, hold it up and tell me the letter name.
Then put the card on the table and search for another card. When you
have found all 26 of the cards, put them in alphabetical order on the table.

WALK-ON AUTUMN ALPHABET LEAVES

PURPOSE: Letter recognition and alphabetical order

MATERIALS: red, orange, brown, and yellow construction paper
scissors
permanent black felt-tip marker
clear Con-Tact paper

PREPARATION: Cut out 26 leaves from orange, brown, yellow, and red construction paper. Print a different letter of the alphabet on each leaf.
Arrange the letters on the classroom floor in alphabetical order in a
stepping stone fashion, as illustrated. Cover each leaf with clear Con-Tact
paper, using enough Con-Tact paper so that the leaf is fully protected by
the plastic and so that the Con-Tact paper attaches the leaf to the floor.

Variation: Instead of autumn leaves, you can use pumpkins, turkeys,
snowflakes, hearts, Easter eggs, or flowers, depending upon the season.

PROCEDURE: The students step on the leaves in order, naming the letter on
each leaf as they step on it.

Variation: This activity can be made into a game for a group of 2–4
students. Students can take turns stepping on the leaves and naming the
letters. The first student continues stepping on leaves until he makes a
mistake naming a letter. If he makes a mistake, he must go back to the

beginning and wait for another turn to try again. It then becomes the next student's turn.

When a student successfully names each of the letters correctly, he becomes a *winner*. To be a *winner,* the student only has to name each letter correctly. He doesn't have to be the first one and he doesn't have to do it on his first try. Thus, it is possible for each of the players to be a winner eventually.

SAY: · On the floor is a set of alphabet leaves. Step on the first leaf, the one with the letter A. Name the letter on the leaf as you step on it. Then name the letter on the next leaf and step on that leaf with your other foot. Continue naming each letter and stepping on each leaf in order.

Walk on the alphabet leaves several times today and often in the next few days.

ALPHABET BOX*

PURPOSE: Letter recognition and alphabetical order

MATERIALS: shallow box with a lid
colored railroad board
permanent black felt-tip marker
a heavy gauge transparency or piece of acetate
scissors
paper cutter

---

*Indicates a self-correcting activity.

PREPARATION: You will need a shallow box with a lid; a gift box would be excellent. Cut a piece of colored railroad board ¼″ smaller than the inside box bottom. Print the letters of the alphabet in alphabetical order on the railroad board. Try to have each letter equally spaced on the railroad board. Mark a big dot in the upper left corner of the railroad board.

Cut a heavy gauge transparency or piece of acetate to the exact size of the railroad board. Place this plastic sheet over the top of the railroad board with the edges exactly lined up. Print each letter onto the plastic, tracing it *exactly* as it is on the railroad board. Mark the dot in the upper lefthand corner.

Next, set the plastic sheet off to the side and cut the railroad board letters apart using a paper cutter. Place the letters and the plastic overlay sheet in the box.

PROCEDURE: This is an individual, independent activity. The student carefully puts the cardboard letters in alphabetical order on the inside bottom of the box.

This activity is self-correcting. The student checks his work when he has finished by putting the plastic overlay sheet on top of the cardboard letters. If the cardboard letters match up with the letters on the plastic overlay, the student knows that the letters are in the right order.

SAY: In this box is a new activity that will help you learn to put the letters of the alphabet in alphabetical order. To do this activity, first remove this plastic sheet and set it off to the side. Now take the cardboard letters out of the box and spread them on the table, letter side up.

Find the letter *a* and place it in the top left corner of the box bottom. Then find the letter *b* and place it next to the letter *a* in the box. Continue putting the cardboard letters in the box in alphabetical order. When you finish one row of letters in the box, start another row of letters, always going from left to right.

When you have placed all of the letters in the correct order, pick up the plastic overlay sheet and set it down in the box over the cardboard letters. Place the plastic sheet so that the dot on the plastic lines up with the dot on the cardboard. If your cardboard letters match up with the letters on the plastic sheet, you will know you have put the letters in the right order. If your cardboard letters do not match exactly with the letters on the plastic sheet, you will know you have made a mistake. Correct any mistakes.

TONGUE DEPRESSOR
ALPHABETICAL ORDER ACTIVITY

PURPOSE: Letter recognition and alphabetical order

MATERIALS: 26 (or 52) tongue depressors
permanent felt-tip marker
box, nut can, or potato chip tube
attractive Con-Tact paper

PREPARATION: You will need 26 tongue depressors (52 tongue depressors if
you want to make a set for both capital and lower case letters). Print a
different letter on each of the 26 tongue depressors. When not in use,
store the tongue depressors in a small box, nut can, or potato chip tube
container covered with attractive Con-Tact paper.

PROCEDURE: Have the student(s) place the tongue depressors in alphabetical
order, as illustrated.

SAY: In this container are 26 tongue depressors. They are like the sticks that the
doctor uses when he looks down your throat. However, each of these has
a letter printed on it. And you should *not put these in your mouth*.

I want you to put the tongue depressors in alphabetical order, one
beneath the other.

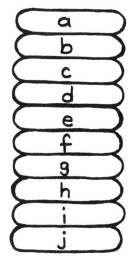

ALPHA-BIT ORDER

PURPOSE: Letter recognition and alphabetical order

MATERIALS: alphabet cereal or alphabet spaghetti

PREPARATION: Pour a pile of alphabet spaghetti or alphabet cereal onto the center of a table.

PROCEDURE: Have the student(s) sort out the letters of the alphabet and put them in alphabetical order.

SAY: On the table is a pile of alphabet spaghetti. Sort out one complete set of letters of the alphabet and place them in a straight line in alphabetical order.

MAGNETIC BOARD ALPHABETICAL ORDER

PURPOSE: Letter recognition and alphabetical order

MATERIALS: magnetic board(s)
             set(s) of plastic magnetic letters

PREPARATION: Place letters in a pile in the center of a table. If the classroom has a magnetic chalkboard, place the letters in a random order on a section of the chalkboard.

PROCEDURE: Have the student(s) select letters and put them in alphabetical order on the magnetic board(s).

SAY: Here is a magnetic board and a set of plastic magnetic letters. The letters are all mixed up. Put the letters on your magnetic board in alphabetical order.

ALPHABET BUTTONS

PURPOSE: Letter recognition and alphabetical order

MATERIALS: 26 (or 52) large plain buttons
             permanent felt-tip marker
             a small box, nut can, or potato chip container
             attractive Con-Tact paper

PREPARATION: You will need 26 large plain buttons (26 buttons of one color and 26 buttons of another color if you want a set for both capital and lower case letters).

Print a different letter on each of the 26 buttons as illustrated.

When not in use, store the alphabet buttons in a small box, nut can or potato chip container covered with attractive Con-Tact paper.

PROCEDURE: Have the student(s) put the buttons in alphabetical order.

SAY: Put the buttons in alphabetical order, one beside the other. Put all of the buttons back into this container when you are finished.

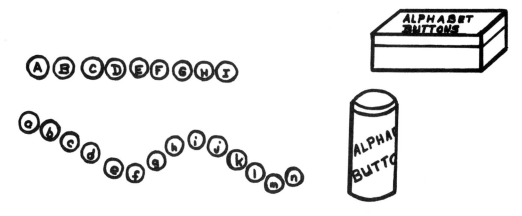

TYPEWRITER ALPHABET FUN

PURPOSE: Letter recognition and alphabetical order

MATERIALS: an old typewriter
             paper

PREPARATION: None

PROCEDURE: Let the students practice finding the letters on the typewriter and typing them in alphabetical order.

SAY: Here is a real typewriter on which you may practice finding letters of the alphabet. Roll in a sheet of paper, like this . . . (demonstrate). Then type the letters in alphabetical order.

PEGBOARD ALPHABET BOARD

PURPOSE: Letter recognition, alphabetical order and matching capital with lower case letters.

MATERIALS: pegboard, 14″ × 20″ or larger
             paint and paintbrush (optional)

26 pegboard hooks
52 one-inch key tags (can be purchased at office supply stores)
permanent red felt-tip marker
permanent blue felt-tip marker
paper punch

PREPARATION: Paint the surface of the pegboard, if needed.

Put the pegboard hooks into the pegboard in rows, spacing the hooks so that there are at least 2 empty holes between hooks and at least 3 empty rows between each row of hooks.

Using a permanent red felt-tip marker, print a different capital letter on each of 26 of the key tags. Then, using a blue felt-tip marker, print a different lower case letter on each of the remaining 26 key tags. If the holes in the key tags are too small to fit onto the hooks, enlarge the holes by punching them with a paper punch.

PROCEDURE: Have the student(s) hang the letter tags on the pegboard in alphabetical order, placing the capital and lower case form of the letter on the same hook.

Use as an independent activity or a small group activity.

SAY: I have spread tags out, letter side up, on the table. I want you to hang the letter tags on the pegboard in alphabetical order. Place the capital and lower case form of the letter on the same hook.

HANGING OUT THE WASH

PURPOSE: Letter recognition and alphabetical order

MATERIALS: assorted colors of construction paper or railroad board
scissors
watercolor black felt-tip marker
laminating materials or clear Con-Tact paper
26 spring-type clothespins
heavy string

PREPARATION: Cut out 26 items of clothing (dresses, trousers, shirts, etc.) from various colors of construction paper or railroad board. Put a different letter of the alphabet on each of the 26 items of clothing. Laminate or cover with clear Con-Tact paper.

Extend a piece of heavy string between two points to form a clothesline. You will also need 26 spring-type clothespins.

PROCEDURE: Have the student(s) hang the clothes on the clothesline in alphabetical order as illustrated.

SAY: Children, I have put up a clothesline and set out some clothespins. I have a big wash I want you to hang out on the clothesline. Clip the clothes in alphabetical order onto the clothesline with these clothespins.

ALPHA-ORDER FISHING

PURPOSE: Letter recognition and alphabetical order

MATERIALS: assorted colors of construction paper or railroad board
scissors
watercolor felt-tip markers
10 feet of heavy string
26 spring-type clothespins
long, sturdy stick

PREPARATION: Cut 26 fish out of construction paper or railroad board. Print a different letter of the alphabet on each fish.

Starting at one end, tie spring-type clothespins to the string at intervals of approximately 4″, until 26 clothespins are tied onto the string. Tie the other end to a stick.

PROCEDURE: Have the student(s) "hook" (clip) the fish onto the line in alphabetical order.

Let the students work on the activity individually or in pairs.

SAY: Today you are going to go fishing! Here is a fishing rod with 26 hooks on its line. You are to "hook" (clip) the fish onto the line in alphabetical order.

ALPHABET FOLLOW-THE-DOT ACTIVITY CARDS

PURPOSE: Letter recognition

MATERIALS: alphabet follow-the-dot books
paper cutter
rubber cement
sheets of 9″ × 12″ oaktag

laminating materials or clear Con-Tact paper
washable transparency marking pens, grease pencils or china
marking pencils
paper towels

PREPARATION: Inexpensive alphabet follow-the-dot books can be found in
toy departments, drug stores and even grocery stores. These can be used
to make good activity cards. Tear out the pages. Trim the pages with a
paper cutter. Glue each page onto 9″ × 12″ sheets of oaktag. Laminate or
cover with clear Con-Tact paper.
You will also need a number of grease pencils, china marking pencils, or washable transparency marking pens.

PROCEDURE: Have the students follow the dots in alphabetical order to draw
the picture on the card.

SAY: Here is a set of Alphabet Follow-the-Dot Cards. Choose a card and a
special marking pencil. Using the special marking pencil, follow the dots
in alphabetical order to draw the picture on the card. When you are
finished, wipe off the picture with paper towel. Then return the card to the
table for someone else to do.
You may do an Alphabet Follow-the-Dot Card whenever you have
finished your other work.

ALPHABET PUZZLE

PURPOSE: Letter recognition and alphabetical order

MATERIALS: shallow box with lid, approximately 9″ × 12″
colored railroad board or posterboard
attractive picture the size of the box
rubber cement
ruler
felt-tip marker
laminating materials or clear Con-Tact paper
scissors

PREPARATION: You will need a shallow box with a lid. Cut a piece of colored
railroad board or posterboard to a rectangular shape to fit easily inside the
box lid. Now find an attractive picture the same size as the piece of
railroad board. Glue the picture to the back side of the piece of railroad
board. Divide the front side of the railroad board into 26 sections, using a

---

*Indicates a self-correcting activity.

ruler and a felt-tip marker. In alphabetical order, print a different letter in each section.

Laminate or cover both sides with clear Con-Tact paper. Cut the 26 sections apart.

PROCEDURE: Have the student put the puzzle back together in the lid of the box by putting the letters in alphabetical order. When finished, have the student place the box *bottom* over the top of the puzzle (inside the box lid), grasp in both hands, pressing the box bottom to the lid, and flip the box and lid over. Then have the student put the box on the table and lift off the lid.

This activity is self-correcting. If the puzzle has been worked correctly, with the letters in the correct alphabetical order, when the lid is lifted off the picture will be exposed with all parts in the correct position.

SAY: Put the puzzle together *in the lid of the box* by putting the letters in alphabetical order. When you have finished, place the box *bottom* on top of the puzzle (inside the box lid). Grasp carefully in both hands, pressing the box bottom to the lid, and flip the box and lid over. (Demonstrate.) Put the box on the table and lift off the lid.

If the puzzle has been worked correctly, with the letters in the correct alphabetical order, when the lid is lifted off, the picture will be exposed with all its parts in the correct position!

STRING THE LETTERS

PURPOSE: Letter recognition and alphabetical order

MATERIALS: 26 plastic or wooden beads (one color)
26 plastic or wooden beads (another color)
2 long shoelaces
permanent black felt-tip marker
box
attractive Con-Tact paper

PREPARATION: You will need 52 wooden or plastic beads with holes through the centers. Beads like this can be purchased through school supply catalogs or from craft and hobby stores. You will need 26 beads of one color and 26 beads of another color. You will also need 2 long shoelaces. Each shoelace must be long enough to string 26 of the beads. Tie a knot in one end of each shoelace.

Print a capital letter on each of the beads of one color. On each of the beads of the other color, print a lower case letter. Cover a box with attractive Con-Tact paper and use it to store the beads and shoelaces.

PROCEDURE: Have the student(s) string the capital letters in alphabetical order on one shoelace and the lower case letters in alphabetical order on the other shoelace. (See the illustration.)

Variation: The students can string the capital letter, then the lower case letter, of the letters A–M in alphabetical order on one shoelace, and the letters N–Z on the other shoelace.

SAY: In this box is a set of alphabet beads. String the capital letters in alphabetical order on one shoelace. String the lower case letters in alphabetical order on the other shoelace.

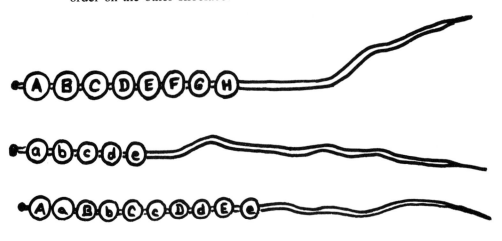

SOLDIERS MARCHING IN A ROW

PURPOSE: Letter recognition and alphabetical order

MATERIALS: oaktag or railroad board
colored pencils, crayons, and/or washable felt-tip markers
scissors
manila envelope
laminating materials (optional)

PREPARATION: Out of oaktag or railroad board, cut 26 typical toy wooden soldiers. Draw in features and color appropriately. Print a different letter of the alphabet on the chest of each soldier.

Draw a soldier on the front of a manila envelope. Print the name of the activity, Soldiers Marching in a Row, across the top of the envelope.

If desired, laminate the soldiers and the manila envelope with its flap open. Slit open the opening to the manila envelope. Store the soldiers in the envelope when not in use.

Note: To make this activity self-correcting, put the soldiers in alphabetical order, then number each card in 1-2-3 order. When students have finished putting the soldiers in alphabetical order, they can turn the soldiers over to check their accuracy.

PROCEDURE: Have the student(s) line the soldiers up along the chalk holder of the chalkboard, one beside the other in alphabetical order.

SAY: Children, today I am going to put a new activity on the activity table. You can select the new activity whenever you have some free time.

Our new activity is called Soldiers Marching in a Row. In the envelope are 26 soldiers (pull out the soldiers), one for each letter of the alphabet. Each soldier has a different letter printed on his chest.

You are to line the soldiers up along the chalkholder of the chalkboard, one beside the other in alphabetical order.

ALPHABET ALLIGATOR*

PURPOSE: Letter recognition and alphabetical order

MATERIALS: green railroad board or posterboard
scissors
black felt-tip marker
laminating materials (optional)
box
attractive Con-Tact paper

PREPARATION: Out of the green railroad board or posterboard, cut an alligator with an extremely long middle. (See the illustration.) Cut the alligator's body into 26 sections. You may need to cut another length of the alligator's middle from the railroad board or posterboard to make the alligator long enough to make the 26 sections. Print a capital letter on each of the 26 sections. Laminate, if desired.

Put the pieces of the alligator into a box covered with attractive Con-Tact paper.

PROCEDURE: Have the student(s) put the alligator together by putting the body sections in alphabetical order.

This activity is self-correcting. If the body parts are not put together in alphabetical order, the body parts will not fit together correctly.

SAY: Here is Alphabet Alligator. He is a puzzle you will enjoy putting together. Put the alligator's head on your left and the alligator's tail on your right.

---

*Indicates a self-correcting activity.

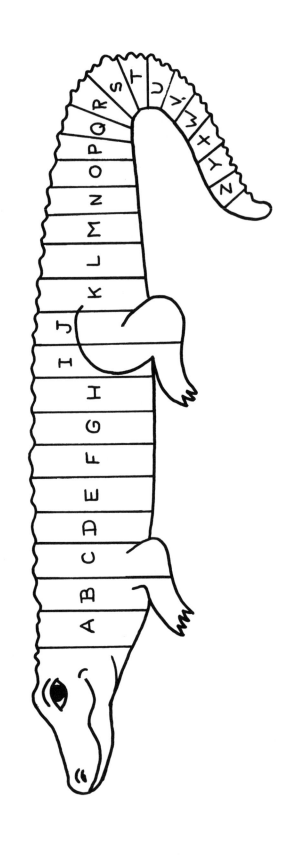

Then put his body together by putting the body sections in alphabetical order. If the parts of the alligators fit together correctly, you will know you have put the letters in the right order. If the parts of his body do not fit together exactly, you will know you have made a mistake. Correct any mistakes.

*LONG, LONG ALPHABET FISH**

PURPOSE: Letter recognition and alphabetical order

MATERIALS: blue railroad board or blue posterboard
scissors
permanent black felt-tip marker
laminating materials (optional)
box
attractive Con-Tact paper

PREPARATION: Out of the blue railroad board or posterboard, cut a fish with an extremely long middle. (See the illustration.) Cut the fish's body into 26 sections. You may need to cut another section of the fish's middle from the railroad board or posterboard to make the fish long enough to make the 26 sections. Print the lower case letters in alphabetical order, one letter to each of the 26 sections. Laminate, if desired.

Put the pieces of the fish into a box covered with attractive Con-Tact paper.

PROCEDURE: Have the student(s) put the fish puzzle together by putting the body sections in alphabetical order.

This activity is self-correcting. The body parts will not fit together properly unless the parts are in alphabetical order.

SAY: In this box is a puzzle called Long, Long Alphabet Fish. You will enjoy putting it together often.

Put the fish's head on your left and the fish's tail on your right. Then put his body together by putting the body sections in alphabetical order.

If the parts of the fish's body fit together exactly, you will know that you have put the letters in the correct order. If they do not fit together exactly, you will know that you have made a mistake. Please correct any mistakes you may make.

---

*Indicates a self-correcting activity.

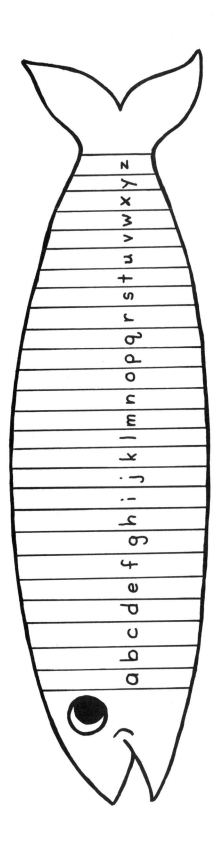

PLASTIC SPOON PARADE

PURPOSE: Letter recognition and alphabetical order

MATERIALS: 26 plastic spoons
permanent felt-tip marker

PREPARATION: Print a different letter of the alphabet on each spoon. (See the illustration.)

PROCEDURE: Have the student(s) line the spoons up in alphabetical order.

SAY: Today I am going to let you take turns organizing a spoon parade. Here are our spoons. You are to line them up in a parade line, one beside the other, in alphabetical order. When you have finished, I will come look at your parade to make sure that your spoons are in the correct order. Then you may mix up the spoons and place them in a pile ready for another student to line up for a parade.

ROLL ACROSS

PURPOSE: Oral alphabetical order

MATERIALS: 1 rubber playground ball, 6″ in diameter or larger

PREPARATION: None

PROCEDURE: The students form a circle. The teacher rolls the ball to a student in the circle. As the teacher rolls the ball, he or she names a letter. The student who catches the ball must repeat the letter named by the teacher and name the next letter of the alphabet. That student then rolls the ball to another student as he or she names a letter of the alphabet.

SAY: We are going to play a new game today. Let's stand in a large circle. I have a ball. I am going to roll it to someone in the circle. As I roll it I am going to name a letter of the alphabet. When the person to whom I roll the ball catches it, he is to repeat the letter I said, then name the next letter of the alphabet. He can then roll the ball to someone else and, as he rolls it, he can name any letter he chooses. We will continue the game in this way.

Let's make sure everyone gets at least one turn catching and rolling the ball.

PUT THE ENCYCLOPEDIAS IN ORDER (I)

PURPOSE: Letter recognition and alphabetical order

MATERIALS: red or blue construction paper
9″ × 12″ sheet of railroad board
3 strips of railroad board, each ½″ × 12″
washable fine felt-tip marker
transparent tape
laminating materials
scissors

PREPARATION: Cut out 26 book-shaped pieces from red or blue construction paper. (See the illustration.) With a washable fine felt-tip pen, draw in book markings on each piece. Print a different capital letter on each "volume."

Tape each of the railroad board strips onto the larger board. The first strip should be taped 3″ from the top of the card, the second strip 6″ from the top, and the third strip along the bottom of the card. Tape only along the bottom and edges of the strips. These strips will be pockets representing shelves on a bookcase. The encyclopedias will be placed "on" these "shelves" in alphabetical order.

Laminate the bookcases and the volumes. Carefully slit open the plastic along the top of each strip. Do not slit the sides.

PROCEDURE: Have the student(s) put the encyclopedias on the shelves in alphabetical order.

SAY: When we were in the school library, we looked at a set of encyclopedias. We talked about what we could find inside of encyclopedias. We saw how each book of the set is kept in a special order. Who can remember in what order the books were kept? . . . That's right. They are kept in alphabetical order.

Today I am going to let you put a little set of encyclopedias in alphabetical order. You may work on it by yourself or with one other friend. Here is our bookcase and here are our little encyclopedias. Each volume of the encyclopedia has a letter on it.

First spread out all of the volumes. Find the one that has the letter A on it. Slide it into the top shelf on the left-hand side. Then find the volume with the letter B on it. Slide it onto the shelf beside volume A and somewhat overlapping volume A. Continue in this manner. When the top shelf is full, continue on the second shelf, then the third shelf.

When you have finished, ask a friend to help you check it.

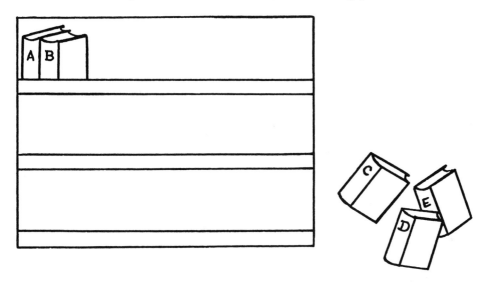

PUT THE ENCYCLOPEDIAS IN ORDER (II)

PURPOSE: Letter recognition and alphabetical order

MATERIALS: set of encyclopedias
masking tape
pair of bookends
sheet of paper
pencil

PREPARATION: You will need a set of encyclopedias. Cover each volume number with a piece of masking tape, leaving the letter name of the volume uncovered. Put the volumes of the encyclopedia on a table in a random order. Put the pair of bookends on the table. Tape a sheet of paper near by and place a pencil near it.

PROCEDURE: The student(s) will put the volumes of encyclopedias in alphabetical order.

SAY: On the table we have a set of encyclopedias. We have talked about how we can look up many kinds of information in an encyclopedia. And we already know that in the Z volume of the encyclopedia we can find out information about things that begin with that letter.

Let's look at this set of encyclopedias. When these encyclopedias are sitting on a shelf, they belong in a certain order. How do we know which book goes first, which one next, etc.? . . . Yes, they are in alphabetical order.

I have mixed up the order of these books. Sometime today I want you to come here and put the encyclopedias in alphabetical order. You may work by yourself or with a friend. When you have finished, ask (name an outstanding student) to come and see if you have put them in alphabetical order correctly. Then write your name on this sheet of paper to let me know that you have put them in order. When you have finished, mix up the order of the books again so that they are ready for another student to work on.

*STRING YOUR FISH**

PURPOSE: Letter recognition and alphabetical order

MATERIALS: assorted colors of railroad board
scissors
permanent felt-tip markers
paper punch
box
attractive Con-Tact paper
shoelace
laminating materials

PREPARATION: Cut 26 fish out of various colors of railroad board. Draw eyes and other appropriate features. Print a different letter on each fish. Use the paper punch to punch a hole in the lower jaw of each fish.

Put the fish in alphabetical order. Write the numerals 1–26 in order, one number on each fish, beginning with *1* on fish *A* and ending with *26* on fish Z. The numerals should be small and on the tail of each fish. No other markings should be on the back side of the fish. Laminate the fish.

Decorate a box with attractive Con-Tact paper. Place fish in the box along with a shoelace with a large knot tied in one end.

---

*Indicates a self-correcting activity.

PROCEDURE: Have the student(s) string the fish on the shoelace in alphabetical order. This activity is self-correcting. When the student has finished stringing the fish on the shoelace in alphabetical order, have the student turn the fish over. If the numerals found on the fish tails are in correct numerical order, the student will know he has put the fish in alphabetical order correctly.

SAY: How many of you have been fishing with your Daddy? When he catches a fish, where does he put it while he catches another fish? Most fishermen put the fish they catch on a stringer. A stringer is a chain or rope with special snaps on it.

First spread the fish out letter side up. String the fish on the stringer in alphabetical order, beginning with the fish with the letter *A* on it.

Today I am going to let you take turns stringing fish on a stringer. Here are the fish. And here is your stringer. (Hold up the shoelace.) It isn't a real stringer but it will work very well for our fish.

First spread the fish out letter side up. String the fish on the stringer in alphabetical order, beginning with the fish with the letter *A* on it.

When you are finished stringing the fish, turn the fish over. If you have put the fish on the stringer in A-B-C order correctly, you will find the numerals 1–26 on the tails of the fish in correct 1-2-3 order. If the fish are not in the right number order, bring up your stringer and we will see what the problem is.

When you have finished stringing the fish, carefully take them off the stringer. Mix the fish up. Then put the fish and the stringer back into the box and put the box back on the activity table ready for another student to use.

BUZZING TO THE HIVE
(A bulletin board activity)

PURPQSE: Letter recognition and alphabetical order

MATERIALS: railroad board
assorted colors of construction paper (including yellow)
scissors
washable black felt-tip marker
washable red felt-tip marker
laminating materials
manila envelope
small box
thumbtacks
tape
bulletin board

PREPARATION: Draw and cut out a beehive from construction paper or railroad board. Tack this to the bulletin board. Add construction paper flowers around the border of the bulletin board. Print the title Buzzing to the Hive. (See the illustration.) Cut 26 bees from yellow construction paper. Draw appropriate markings on both sides of the bees with the washable black felt-tip marker. With the washable red felt-tip marker, print a different capital and matching lower case letter on the wings of both sides of each of the 26 bees.

        Laminate the bees to give them extra strength and durability. Put the bees into a large manila envelope and print instructions on the envelope. Tack and tape a small box containing 30–35 thumbtacks to the bulletin board near the envelope.

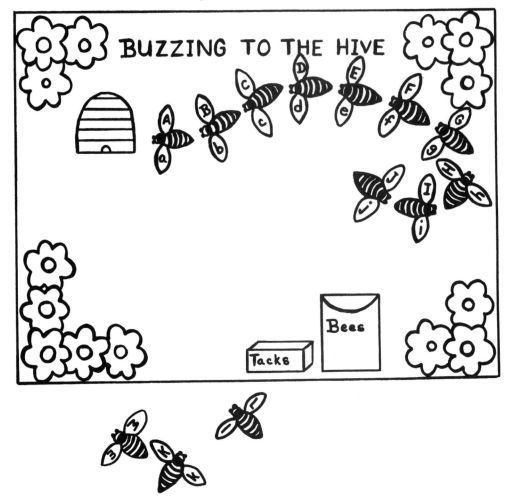

PROCEDURE: Have the students tack the bees in alphabetical order onto the bulletin board. Let the students work on this activity individually.

SAY: On the bulletin board is an activity you may take turns working on. It is called Buzzing To The Hive.

   To do the activity, remove the bees from the envelope and spread them out. Find the bee with the first letter of the alphabet on its wings. Tack it to the bulletin board near the hive as though it were flying to the hive. Continue tacking each bee, one behind the other, in alphabetical order. When you have finished, I will come check your work.

   After I have checked your bees, take them down and put the tacks and the bees back in their containers ready for another student to use.

TRIANGLE TRAIN PUZZLE

PURPOSE: Letter recognition and alphabetical order

MATERIALS: railroad board or posterboard
paper cutter
fine felt-tip marker
laminating materials (optional)
box
attractive Con-Tact paper

PREPARATION: Out of one or more colors of railroad board or posterboard, cut 26 equilateral triangles, with each side approximately 2″ long. Place the triangles side by side, with one triangle pointing up, the next pointing down, up, down, etc. Print a different letter of the alphabet on each triangle, as illustrated. Draw a line under each letter so that the children will know if the letter is right side up. Laminate, if possible. Decorate a box with attractive Con-Tact paper in which to store the puzzle when not in use.

PROCEDURE: Have the student(s) put the puzzle together by putting the triangles in alphabetical order.

SAY: In this box is a puzzle you will enjoy putting together. You will want to put this puzzle together on the floor because you will need lots of room.

   Take out the puzzle pieces and spread them out on the floor, letter side up. Turn all of the pieces so that the lines are under the letters. Find the triangle that has the letter *a* on it. That is your first puzzle piece. Next, find the triangle with the letter *b* on it. Place it next to the *a* with the triangle point down. Find the triangle with *c* on it. Place it next to the *b* triangle with its point pointing up. Continue putting the pieces together in alphabetical order.

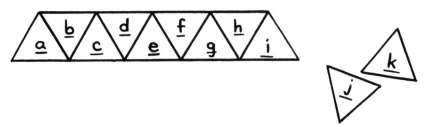

ALPHABETICAL ORDER IN A CARD HOLDER

PURPOSE: Letter recognition and alphabetical order

MATERIALS: unlined 3″ × 5″ file cards, one for each student
26 cards, each 1¼″ × 3″
fine felt-tip marker
transparent tape

PREPARATION: Fold each 3″ × 5″ file card up 1″ across the bottom, crease, and tape at each end to make a pocket. This will be the card holder. Print a different letter on each of the twenty-six 1½″ × 3″ cards.

PROCEDURE: Spread the letter cards on the table letter side down. Give each student in the group a card holder. Students take turns drawing 3 cards from the pile of letter cards and putting them in alphabetical order in their individual card holders.

INTRODUCTION: I am going to give each of you a letter card holder. In the center of the table are cards with letters printed on them. The letters are facing down. When it is your turn, draw any 3 cards from the center of the table and place them in alphabetical order in your card holder. Then show us your card holder and we will see if we agree that you have them in the correct order. Then you will take the letter cards out of your card holder, put them back in the pile and mix up the cards in the pile. It will then be the next person's turn to do the same. You will each have several turns.

CRAZY CATERPILLAR

PURPOSE: Letter recognition and alphabetical order.

MATERIALS: red railroad board or construction paper
permanent black felt-tip marker

> scissors
> compass
> laminating materials (optional)
> small box
> attractive Con-Tact paper

PREPARATION: Cut 26 circles, approximately 1½″ in diameter, from the red railroad board or construction paper. Print a different letter of the alphabet on each circle. Then cut a catepillar head slightly larger than the circles and draw features. Laminate all pieces, if desired.

Decorate a small box with attractive Con-Tact paper. Keep the catepillar parts in the box when not in use.

PROCEDURE: Have the student(s) put the Crazy Catepillar together by putting his body parts in alphabetical order, as illustrated.

SAY: I'd like you to meet a friend of mine. His name is Crazy Caterpillar. He is called Crazy Caterpillar because he looks so funny and because his body keeps coming apart. Crazy Caterpillar lives in this box. Let's see if he is home now. (Peek into the box.) Yes, he's home. But I should have known, his body has come apart again! (Open the box up all the way and show the contents to the students.) Let's see if we can find his head. Here it is. Let's spread out his body pieces, letter side up. The piece with the letter *a* on it goes right next to the head. The next piece of his body has a *b* on it. And the next has a *c* on it.

I'm going to put Crazy Caterpillar back in his home for now. But whenever you have some free time, you can take turns getting my friend out of his box and putting him together. Remember, his body parts must be put together in alphabetical order.

Be sure to put him back in the box and back on our activity table when you are through putting him together.

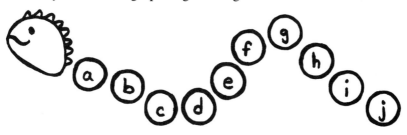

HOP ALONG

PURPOSE: Letter recognition and letter sequence

HOP ALONG !

MATERIALS: 14″ × 22″ sheet of colored railroad board or posterboard
small sheet of colored railroad board
felt-tip markers
laminating materials
paper fastener
paper clip
game markers

PREPARATION: On the 14″ × 22″ sheet of colored railroad board or posterboard, draw a game board as illustrated. Laminate.

To make a spinner for the game, cut out a circle of colored railroad
board from the small sheet. Draw lines dividing this piece into 3 pie-
shaped pieces. Mark each section with a different numeral, 1–3. Laminate. Insert a paper fastener through a paper clip, then on through the
center of the circle. Bend the prongs on the paper fastener flat against the
back side of the spinner, leaving the paper fastener loose enough for the
paper clip to spin easily.

You will also need game markers.

PROCEDURE: The players take turns spinning the spinner and moving their
game markers forward the number of spaces indicated. Each player must
name the letter on the space on which he landed and name the names of
the next 2 letters that come after that letter in the alphabet.

SAY: Players place their markers on the rabbit. The first player spins the spinner and hops his marker forward that number of spaces. He must then
name the letter on the space on which he landed and name the names of
the next 2 letters that come after that letter in the alphabet. It is then the
next player's turn to spin the spinner and move his marker forward.

Any player unable to name the letter on the space on which he landed
or name the next 2 letters in the alphabet, must hop his marker right back
to the space he was on before he spun the spinner for that turn. The
winner is the first player to hop his marker to the vegetables.

WHICH CHEST?

PURPOSE: Capital and lower case letter recognition and alphabetical order

MATERIALS: 16″ × 22″ sheet of railroad board or posterboard
scissors
art knife
3 small manila envelopes
rubber cement

laminating materials or clear Con-Tact paper
yellow railroad board or oaktag
compass
permanent felt-tip markers

PREPARATION: On the sheet of railroad board or posterboard, draw three
treasure chests and label them as illustrated. Carefully cut a straight slot
about 3″ long in the gold coins of each treasure chest.

Cut the flaps off 3 small manila envelopes. Cut a 3″ slot in one side
of each manila envelope. Glue each envelope to the back of the activity
board, lining the slots on the envelopes up with the slots on the activity
board. On the envelope glued behind the treasure chest with the letters
A-I, print the Letters A-I. Print letters that correspond with the other
treasure chests on the other 2 envelopes. Laminate both sides of the
activity board or cover with clear Con-Tact paper. Carefully cut open the
slots and the top opening of each envelope.

Next you will need to make the "gold coins." With a compass, draw
52 circles, each 2″ in diameter, on yellow oaktag or railroad board. Cut
these out. Print a different capital or lower case letter on each.

(Illustration of back of activity board)

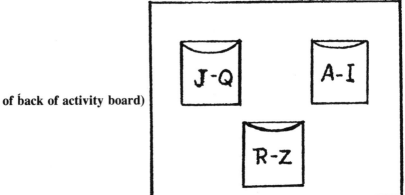

PROCEDURE: Two students may do this activity together. The students take
turns picking up coins, saying the letter name aloud, and deciding in
which chest the coins belong. They slide the coins into the slot of the
appropriate treasure chest. When the students have completed the activity, the teacher should check to see that the coins have been correctly
placed.

Variation: An alternative way of checking accuracy is to have the student list on a sheet of paper the letters on the coins placed in each
envelope. This list can then be given to the teacher to be checked later.

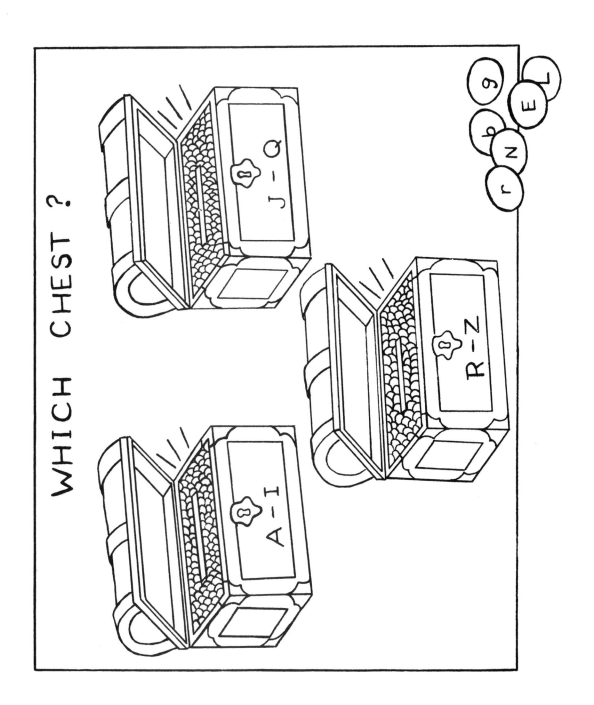

This activity can also be done by an individual child as an independent activity.

SAY: Two students may do this activity together. Place the activity board on a table. Mix up and spread out the coins, letter side down. Take turns picking up coins, saying the letter name aloud, and deciding in which chest the coin belongs. Slide the coin into the slot of the appropriate treasure chest.

When you have finished the activity, I will remove the coins from the first envelope behind the activity board and check to make sure the coins have been correctly placed. I will then check the other 2 envelopes.

ALPHABET FLOWER POWER

PURPOSE: Letter recognition and alphabetical order

MATERIALS: yellow railroad board or posterboard
railroad board of another color
scissors
permanent black felt-tip marker
art knife
laminating materials

PREPARATION: Cut a circle with a diameter of approximately 6″ out of yellow railroad board or posterboard. Carefully cut 26 slots around the circle, staggering the slots. (See the illustration.)

Cut 26 flower petals, each approximately 4½″ long out of one or more contrasting colors of railroad board. Print a different letter of the alphabet on each petal.

Laminate all parts.

PROCEDURE: Have student(s) insert flower petals in alphabetical order into the flower center.

SAY: You may work on our Alphabet Flower by yourself or in pairs. Lay out all of the flower petals letter side up. Select the petal with the first letter of the alphabet and insert it into any slot in the yellow circular flower center. Then select the petal with the second letter of the alphabet and insert that petal into the slot immediately to the right of the first petal. Continue in this manner until you have inserted each of the petals, in correct alphabetical order, into the flower center to form a flower.

When you have completed making the flower, I will check the flower to make sure that you have the petals in alphabetical order. Then you may remove the petals and mix them up so they are ready for another student to do.

STAPLE THEM IN ALPHABETICAL ORDER

PURPOSE: Placing words in alphabetical order

MATERIALS: assorted colors of construction paper
             paper cutter

fine felt-tip marker
stapler and staples

PREPARATION: Cut a number of 1″ × 4″ strips of various colors of construction paper. On one side of each paper strip, print a different 3- or 4-letter word. Have at least one word for each letter of the alphabet. You may need 2 or 3 different words for each letter of the alphabet, depending on the size of the group with which you intend to use this activity.

You will also need a stapler and staples.

PROCEDURE: The students take turns picking up 3 pieces of paper, placing them in alphabetical order, then stapling them together at one end.

SAY: A different word is printed on each piece of paper in my hand. I am going to place these pieces of paper, word side down, in the middle of the table. Let's mix them up well by moving them around.

Who remembers what alphabetical order is? . . . Who remembers how we can put words in alphabetical order? . . . Today we are going to practice putting words in alphabetical order. We are going to take turns picking up 3 pieces of paper, placing them in alphabetical order, then stapling them together at one end. You will each have several turns. And you may keep the word strips you staple together.

PUT THE CLASS IN ORDER

PURPOSE: Alphabetical order

MATERIALS: colored 3″ × 5″ file cards
paper cutter or scissors
fine felt-tip marker

PREPARATION: Cut colored 3″ × 5″ file cards in half so that you have one 2½″ × 3″ card for each student in the class. Print the first name of each child in the class on the cards, one name on each card. If more than one student has the same first name, print their first names plus the first letter of their last names.

Note: To make the activity self-correcting, put the names in alphabetical order by the first names. Then turn the cards over and number each card in numerical order.

PROCEDURE: Have the student put the name cards in alphabetical order. When finished, the student can check his accuracy by turning the cards over and checking to see if they are in numerical order.

SAY: Here is a set of cards with the names of each of the children in this class on them. When you have an opportunity, get the set of cards and put the names in alphabetical order. When there are 2 first names exactly the same, you will see the first letter of the last name. When there are 2 first names the same, you will have to look at the first letter of the last name to decide which of the names comes first in alphabetical order.

When you have finished putting them in alphabetical order, turn them over. You will see numbers on the back of the cards. If the cards are in correct alphabetical order, the numbers on the back of the cards will be in 1-2-3 order. If the numbers are out of order, you have not put the names in correct alphabetical order.

FILE THE WORDS

PURPOSE: Alphabetical order

MATERIALS: $3'' \times 5''$ file card box
$3'' \times 5''$ alphabetical file divider cards
$3'' \times 5''$ file cards or pieces of paper
fine felt-tip marker

PREPARATION: Put the alphabetical file divider cards into the file box in correct alphabetical order.

Print a different word on each file card or piece of paper. Have several words for some of the more common letters. The number of word cards you want to make will depend upon the level and skill of the students with whom you plan to use the activity.

PROCEDURE: Have the student(s) file the word cards in the box in alphabetical order by placing each card behind the correct letter divider card.

Note: Younger students or children having difficulty can place the word cards using the first letter of the word only. More advanced children should be instructed to refer to the second or third letter of the word to determine proper placement of words beginning with the same letter.

SAY: Beside this box are word cards. File the word cards in the box in alphabetical order by placing each card behind the correct letter divider card.

GOOD LUCK!

PURPOSE: Alphabetical letter sequence

MATERIALS: 9″ × 12″ sheet of dark green railroad board or posterboard
lighter green construction paper
rubber cement
scissors
fine felt-tip black marker
laminating materials or clear Con-Tact paper
washable transparency marking pens or grease pencil
paper towels

PREPARATION: Cut approximately 12 four-leaf clovers out of the green construction paper. Glue the clovers onto the dark green railroad board or
posterboard. Print one letter on each clover, leaving dashes where letters
are to be filled in by the student. (See the illustration.) Laminate or cover
with clear Con-Tact paper.

You will also need a grease pencil or a washable transparency marking pen.

PROCEDURE: Have the students use the washable transparency marking pen to
fill in the three letters that come after the letter given on a clover. When
the student has finished filling in the missing letters on all of the clover
leaves, he wipes the activity card off with a paper towel so that it is ready
to be used by another student.

SAY: How many of you have found four-leaf clovers? Why is it special when
you find a four-leaf clover? . . . This activity board has many four-leaf
clovers on it. At the top it says Good Luck! You will need to do good
thinking when you work on this activity. When you have finished it, if
your work is correct, you will have had ''good luck.''

You will use this special marking pencil when you work on this activity. On the first clover is the letter *r*. What are the 3 letters of the alphabet that come *after* the letter *r*? Print those letters, one on each clover leaf, in alphabetical order going in this direction (demonstrate using a clockwise direction). Go on to another clover. Decide what letters come after the letter that is given. Then print those letters in order on the clover leaves. Do all of the clovers in this way. When you have finished, let me check your card.

You will want to work on this activity by yourself. After I have checked your card, you may wipe your answers off with a paper towel. Then put the activity card and the special pencil back on the table ready for another student to use.

CIRCLE FILL-IN

PURPOSE: Alphabet letter sequence

MATERIALS: assorted colors of construction paper or railroad board
washable fine felt-tip marker
compass
laminating materials or clear Con-Tact paper
scissors
washable transparency marking pen or a grease pencil
paper towels

PREPARATION: Cut 20–30 circles out of various colors of construction paper or railroad board. Print on each circle 1–2 letters and draw 1–2 lines indicating blanks where letters are to be supplied by the students. (See the illustration.) Laminate or cover with clear Con-Tact paper.

You will also need a washable transparency marking pen or a grease pencil.

PROCEDURE: Have the student use the washable transparency marking pen or a grease pencil-to fill in the missing letters on each circle. After the student has completed the activity, the letters are wiped off with a paper towel ready for another student to use.

This is an activity for the students to do individually.

SAY: On each of these circles you will see letters and several blanks. You will use this special marking pencil to fill in the missing letters on each circle. Print a missing letter in each blank. If the circle had the letter *A*, then two blanks, what are the next two letters after *A*? . . . Right, the next two letters are *B* and *C*. You would print those 2 letters in the blanks.

If the two blanks are before the letter, think what two letters come before that letter. Then print them in the blanks. Fill in the missing letters on the rest of the circles in the same way.

When you have finished the circles, I will check them with you. Then you may get a paper towel and wipe off your answers. The circles will then be ready for another student to use.

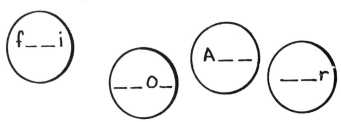

RING THE BELLS

PURPOSE: Alphabet letter sequence

MATERIALS: colored construction paper
9″ × 12″ sheet of oaktag or railroad board
rubber cement
black fine felt-tip marker
laminating materials
scissors
washable transparency marking pen or a grease pencil

PREPARATION: Cut bells out of colored construction paper. Glue them onto the sheet of oaktag or railroad board in clusters of 2, 3 or 4. Print the title of the activity, Ring the Bells, at the top of the board. Print one letter on one bell of each cluster, as illustrated. Laminate.

You will also need a grease pencil or a washable transparency marking pen.

PROCEDURE: In each group of bells, one letter is given. The student thinks of what letters come before that letter or after that letter in the alphabet. Then he uses the transparency marking pen or the grease pencil to fill in the missing letters on the blank bells. When the activity has been completed and checked, the student wipes off his answers with a paper towel.

SAY: Here is an activity card you may work on by yourself when you have finished doing your other work. It is called Ring the Bells. In each group of bells, one letter is given. Think of what letters come before that letter or after that letter in the alphabet. Fill in the missing letters on the blank bells. Write the missing letters using this special marking pencil.

When you have completed the activity card, bring it to me to check. Then wipe off your answers with a paper towel. The activity card will then be ready for someone else to do.

BANANA CARDS*

PURPOSE: Alphabet letter sequence

MATERIALS: yellow railroad board
fine felt-tip marker
red fine felt-tip marker
laminating materials or clear Con-Tact paper
scissors
box
attractive Con-Tact paper
washable transparency marking pen or grease pencil

PREPARATION: Cut bananas approximately 6″ long from yellow railroad board. On each banana print sets of dashes and letters, as illustrated. Each banana should have different letters and blanks.

---

*Indicates a self-correcting activity.

This activity is self-correcting. On the back of each banana print the letters found on that banana, with the missing letters filled in in red and underlined. Laminate or cover with clear Con-Tact paper.

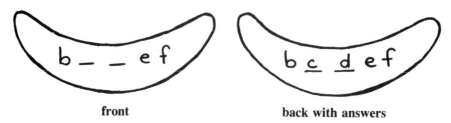

front   **back with answers**

You will also need a washable transparency marking pen or a grease pencil.

Decorate a box in which to keep the banana cards and special marker when not in use.

PROCEDURE: Have the student fill in the missing letters on each of the banana cards using the transparency marking pen. When the student finishes filling in the missing letters, he should turn the banana cards over to check his answers. When the student has finished all the banana cards, he should wipe his answers off thoroughly with a paper towel so the cards are ready for use by another student.

SAY: Here is a set of activity cards called Banana Cards. They will let you practice printing letters and remembering which letter comes after which letter. You may work on them by yourself or with a friend.

You will need to use this special marking pen to mark on the cards. Select a banana card and print the missing letters in in the blanks. When you have finished, turn the card over and check your answers. Then do another banana card. When you have finished all of the banana cards and checked each one, wipe your answers off thoroughly with a paper towel. Then put the bananas and special markers back into their box and place them on the shelf ready for another student to use.

HIPPOPOTAMUS FILL-INS

PURPOSE: Letter formation and alphabetical order

MATERIALS: assorted colors of railroad board or oaktag
scissors
permanent felt-tip markers
laminating materials or clear Con-Tact paper

washable transparency marking pens or grease pencils
paper towels

PREPARATION: Out of assorted colors of oaktag or railroad board, cut 5–6 hippopotamuses, each approximately 4½" × 8". Draw features on each hippo. (See the illustration.) On each card print sets of dashes and letters, as illustrated. Each hippo should have different letters and blanks. On the back of each card write a different numeral so that the students will have a way of telling which cards they have done. Laminate or cover with clear Con-Tact paper.

You will also need several grease pencils or washable transparency marking pens.

PROCEDURE: Have students use the washable transparency marking pens to fill in the missing letters on the Hippopotamus Fill-In Cards. After the teacher has checked the cards, the students should wipe off their answers so the cards will be ready for other students to fill in.

SAY: Here are 6 different hippopotamus activity cards you may work on. You will need to use one of these special marking pens to mark on these cards. Select a hippopotamus card. Print the missing letters in each blank. When you have finished, print your name on the card and place it on my desk. I will check it with you as soon as I have time. After we have checked your card, wipe off your answers with a paper towel. Then return it to the activity table and select another hippopotamus card to work on.

Each hippopotamus card has a different numeral printed on the back of it. You may wish to write on a sheet of paper the numbers of the hippo cards as you complete them. Then you will be able to easily figure out which cards you have not yet done.

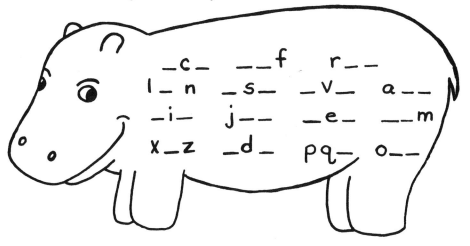

LETTER FAN

PURPOSE: Letter recognition, differentiating between capital and lower case
letters, and alphabetical order

MATERIALS: one or more colors of railroad board
permanent felt-tip markers
scissors
laminating materials
paper punch
1 notebook ring
box

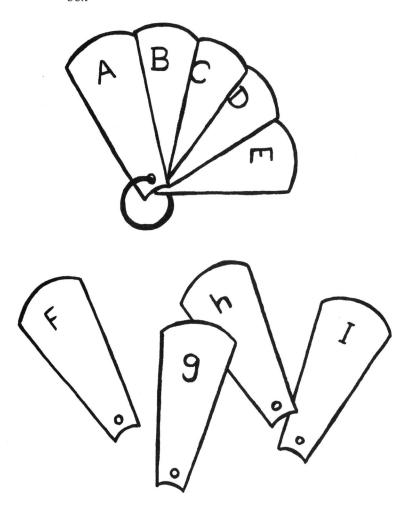

PREPARATION: Cut 26 sections of fan out of one or more colors of railroad
board. Each piece should be approximately 4″ long and shaped as illustrated. Print a different letter of the alphabet on each of the 26 pieces,
printing the capital letter on one side and the lower case form of the letter
on the reverse side. Laminate.

With the paper punch, punch a hole in the small end of each fan
piece.

You will need one notebook ring, available from school and office
supply stores.

PROCEDURE: Have the student(s) place the fan sections on the open notebook
ring in alphabetical order, with all capital letters facing one direction and
all lower case letters the other direction.

SAY: Sometime today you may put together our Letter Fan. To put it together,
place the fan sections on the open notebook ring in alphabetical order,
with all capital letters facing one direction and all lower case letters the
other direction. When you have finished, clamp the notebook ring shut.
Then fan out the sections of the fan and read the letters to a friend or to
me.

Then remove the fan sections from the ring, mix them up and put
them in this box ready for another student.

ALPHABET PAPER CHAIN

PURPOSE: Letter recognition and alphabetical order

MATERIALS: colored construction paper
paper cutter
washable black felt-tip marker
white school glue

PREPARATION: Cut colored construction paper into strips approximately 1″
wide. You will need 26 strips for each student in the group. In the center
of each of the 26 strips, print a different letter of the alphabet. Give one
set of 26 strips to each student in the group.

Each student will need a bottle of glue.

PROCEDURE: Have the students make paper chains by gluing the strips in
interlocking loops in alphabetical order.

SAY: How many of you have made paper chains at Christmas time? Today we
are going to make paper chains, but not for Christmas decorations. We

are going to make paper chains to practice our alphabet! I am going to give each of you 26 strips of paper. You will need to get out your own bottles of glue.

First, spread out your letter strips with the letter side up. Find the strip with the letter *a* on it. Put a small amount of glue on one end of the strip. Make a loop, like this (demonstrate), and stick the two ends together. Hold them together for a few seconds. Next, find the strip with the letter *b*. Make it into a loop going through the first loop and glue the ends together. (Demonstrate.) Continue doing this with *c,* then *d,* etc., being sure to put the letters in alphabetical order, and being sure that the letter is facing toward you and is right side up.

WHICH SNOWDRIFT?

PURPOSE: Capital and lower case letter recognition and alphabetical order

MATERIALS: 14″ × 22″ sheet of royal blue railroad board
white felt-tip marker (substitute white tempera paint or white shoe polish, if necessary)
black felt-tip marker
art knife
3 small manila envelopes
rubber cement
laminating materials or clear Con-Tact paper
heavy white paper
scissors

PREPARATION: Use the white felt-tip marker to print Which Snow Drift? across the top of the blue railroad board. Then draw some snowflakes, snow, and 3 snowdrifts, as illustrated. With the black felt-tip marker, print A-I, J-R and S-Z on the snowdrifts. Carefully cut a straight slot about 3″ long in each snowdrift.

Cut the flaps off 3 small manila envelopes. Cut a 3″ slot in one side of each manila envelope. Glue each envelope to the back of the activity board, lining the slots on the envelopes up with the slots on the activity board. On the envelope behind the drift with the letters A-I, print the letters A-I. Print the letters that correspond with the other snowdrifts on the other two envelopes.

Laminate both sides of the activity board or cover with clear Con-Tact paper. Then, carefully cut open the slots and the top opening of each envelope.

Next, cut snowflakes out of heavy white paper. Print on each a different capital or lower case letter.

PROCEDURE: The student slides snowflakes into the slot in the appropriate snowdrift.

SAY: Here is a good activity to give you practice with the letters of the alphabet. Place the activity board on a table and spread out the snowflakes letter side up. Pick up a snowflake and decide in which drift it belongs. Slide the snowflake into the slot in the appropriate snowdrift. (Demonstrate.) Continue placing each snowflake into the correct snowdrift. When you have finished, I will turn the activity board over, remove the snowflakes from the envelopes, and check to make sure that you have put the snowflakes into the correct snowdrifts.

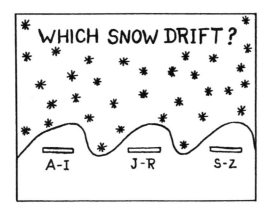

PUMPKIN PATCH

(A bulletin board activity)

PURPOSE: Letter recognition and alphabetical order

MATERIALS: brown kraft paper
gold kraft paper
assorted colors of felt-tip markers (including brown)
scissors
bulletin board
black kraft paper
brown, yellow, and orange construction paper
green tempera paint
paintbrush
paper punch
rubber cement
thumbtacks
stapler and staples
laminating materials

PREPARATION: Cover a bulletin board with brown kraft paper. Print Pumpkin Patch across the top of the board. Cut a corn shock out of gold kraft paper. Use a brown felt-tip marker to draw some lines on the corn shock to make it look more realistic. Staple it to the lower left corner of the bulletin board.

Out of black kraft paper, cut a gnarled tree with branches without leaves. Staple it in the upper right area of the bulletin board.

Cut an owl out of dark brown construction paper. Cut two large eyes out of yellow construction paper. Glue the eyes onto the owl. Staple the owl onto a tree branch.

Cut 26 pumpkins out of orange construction paper. Print a different letter of the alphabet on each pumpkin. Laminate the pumpkins. Punch a hole near the top of each pumpkin with a paper punch. Tack the pumpkins to the bulletin board in a random order, putting the thumbtacks through the holes in the pumpkins.

With green tempera paint, paint a vine with several leaves on the brown background paper.

PROCEDURE: Have the students take turns naming the letters on the pumpkins. The teacher names a student and points to a pumpkin. The student names the letter on the pumpkin.

Note: When the students have finished the above activity, take the pumpkins off the bulletin board. Then let the students take turns tacking the pumpkins to the bulletin board in alphabetical order. They can do this activity individually or in pairs in their spare time.

Variation: To make this into an activity to work on matching capital with lower case letters, print the lower case form of each letter on the top half of the pumpkin. Print the corresponding capital letter on the bottom half of each pumpkin. Cut each pumpkin in half. Staple the top half of each pumpkin along the vine in a random order.

Have the students take turns, independently or in pairs, tacking the bottoms of the pumpkins onto the bulletin board so that the capital letters match the lower case letters.

This activity is self-correcting because each pumpkin is a somewhat different size or shape and each pumpkin bottom will fit only one pumpkin top.

SAY: We have a new bulletin board for Halloween. It is called Pumpkin Patch. We are going to take turns naming the letters on the pumpkins. When I call your name, you name the letter on the pumpkin to which I point.

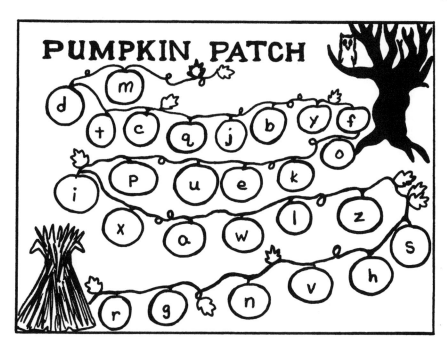

Variation

VALENTINE PAPER CLIP BOARD*

PURPOSE: Alphabetical order

MATERIALS: 16″ × 20″ sheet of white tagboard
18″ × 22″ sheet of red railroad board
art knife
rubber cement
laminating materials
red construction paper
26 paper clips
washable black felt-tip marker
scissors

PREPARATION: Cut 26 well-spaced ½″ slits in the white tagboard. Center the tagboard on the railroad board and glue the *edges only* of the tagboard to the railroad board. Laminate, then cut open the slits. Insert one paper clip in each slit.

Cut out 26 hearts from red construction paper. Using the washable black felt-tip marker, print a different letter of the alphabet on each heart. Place the hearts in alphabetical order. On the back of each heart print a numeral very small, 1 on the heart with the letter A, 2 on B, 3 on C, etc. Laminate the hearts.

PROCEDURE: Have the student(s) slide the hearts under the paper clips on the activity board in alphabetical order. This activity can be used as a teacher-directed small group activity or as an individual independent activity.

When the group has completed this activity under teacher direction, instruct the students that they may do the activity individually or in pairs.

This activity is self-correcting. When the students have completed the activity, they can check their accuracy by making sure the numerals on the backs of the hearts are in numerical order.

SAY: Today we are going to use a new type of activity board to practice our letters. This is our Valentine Board. Here are the valentine hearts in my hand. Each heart has a letter of the alphabet on it. Let's spread out the hearts, letter side up, on the table.

Find the heart with the letter A printed on it. Slide that heart under the first paper clip on the activity board. Now we are going to take turns naming the next letter of the alphabet, finding the heart with that letter, and putting that heart under the next paper clip on the activity board.

---

*Indicates a self-correcting activity.

ANIMAL PARADE

PURPOSE: Letter recognition and alphabetical order

MATERIALS: assorted colors of construction paper
scissors
colored pencils
washable fine felt-tip markers
washable wide felt-tip markers
laminating materials or clear Con-Tact paper
sheet of paper
tape
chalkboard

PREPARATION: Out of appropriate colors of construction paper, cut the shapes of 26 different animals. With colored pencils and /or *washable* fine felt-tip markers, draw in some of the animals' features. With a *washable* wide felt-tip marker, print a different letter on the front side of each animal. The letters printed on the animals should be selected at random. The letter printed on an animal should *not* be the same letter with which the animal's name begins. Laminate all of the animals or cover them with clear Con-Tact paper.

Tape a sheet of paper on the chalkboard. Print across the top of the paper I Have Finished the Animal Parade. The children will sign this paper when they have done the activity.

PROCEDURE: The student(s) line the animals up in alphabetical order on the chalk holder of the chalkboard.

SAY: In my hands I have 26 wild animals. On each animal there is a printed letter. You will each have a turn to line these animals up for an animal parade. The animal with the letter *A* on it will be the first animal in the parade. The animal with the letter *B* on it will be the second animal in line. In other words, you will line the animals up, one behind the other, in alphabetical order.

You may work on the animal parade by yourself or with one friend. Line the animals up in order on the chalk holder of the chalkboard, propping them upright against the chalkboard. When you have finished lining them up, ask me to come look at your parade. When I have checked to see that they are indeed in the right order, you may put them in a pile all mixed up ready for another student to put into a parade.

When you have finished the activity, sign your name on this sheet of paper to show me that you have done it.

3

GAMES AND ACTIVITIES TO REINFORCE MATCHING CAPITAL AND LOWER CASE LETTERS

PRINT THE OTHER LETTER CARDS–
LOWER CASE LETTERS

PURPOSE: Letter recognition, letter formation, matching capital and lower
case letters

MATERIALS: assorted colors of construction paper
scissors
laminating materials or clear Con-Tact paper
fine felt-tip marker
washable transparency marking pen or a grease pencil
paper towels

PREPARATION: Cut a free-form shape out of construction paper. Use this as a
pattern to make 26 identical cutout shapes from various colors of construction paper. Print a different capital letter on each shape. Draw a line
to the right of each capital letter. (See the illustration.) Laminate or cover
with clear Con-Tact paper.

You will also need a washable transparency marking pen or a grease
pencil.

PROCEDURE: The student prints the lower case form of the letter on each card
using the special marking pen. When his cards have been checked, he
should wipe off his answers with a paper towel.

SAY: On each of these cards you will see a different capital letter and a line
beside it on which you are to print the lower case form of the letter. Print
the letter using this special marking pencil.

You may take turns working on this activity. Only one person should
do the cards at a time.

When you have finished the cards, bring the cards to me so that I
may check them. Then wipe your answers off with a paper towel. The
cards will then be ready for another student to use.

PRINT THE OTHER LETTER CARDS—
CAPITAL LETTERS

PURPOSE: Letter recognition, letter formation, matching capital with lower case letters

MATERIALS: white tagboard or heavy white art paper
compass
black fine felt-tip marker
laminating materials or clear Con-Tact paper
scissors
washable transparency marking pen or grease pencil
paper towel

PREPARATION: Cut out a circle, approximately 3½″ in diameter. Use this as a pattern to cut out 26 identical circles from white tagboard or heavy white art paper.

Draw in baseball markings on each circle. (See the illustration.) Print a different lower case letter on each baseball card. Draw a line to the left of each lower case letter. Laminate or cover with clear Con-Tact paper.

You will also need a washable transparency marking pen or a grease pencil.

PROCEDURE: The student prints the capital form of the letter on each card using the special marking pen. When his cards have been checked, he should wipe off his answers with a paper towel.

PIN A TAIL ON A RABBIT
(A bulletin board activity)

PURPOSE: Matching capital and lower case letters

MATERIALS: railroad board or construction paper
             assorted colors of fine felt-tip markers
             colored pencils (optional)
             scissors
             heavy white drawing paper or oaktag
             paper punch
             laminating materials (optional)
             box of thumbtacks
             envelope
             bulletin board

PREPARATION: Out of railroad board or construction paper, cut 26 rabbits.
         Mark in some of the features and print a different capital letter on each
         rabbit. Tack the rabbits onto a bulletin board.

         Out of heavy white drawing paper or oaktag, cut 26 rabbit tails. Print
         a different lower case letter on each tail. Using paper punch, punch one
         hole in the top of each tail. Laminate all parts, if desired.

         Tack a box of thumbtacks to the bulletin board. Tack an envelope to
         the bulletin board. Put the rabbit tails in the envelope.

PROCEDURE: Have the student(s) match capital with lower case letters by
         pinning the tails on the correct bunnies.

SAY: On our bulletin board we have a new game. It is called Pin a Tail on a
       Rabbit. There are 26 bunny rabbits on the bulletin board. Each of the
       bunnies has a capital letter printed on it. But each bunny is missing
       something. Who can tell me what is missing? . . . That's right. The
       bunnies are missing their tails.

       In this envelope are the bunny rabbit tails. And in this little box are
       thumbtacks. You are to pin each tail on the right rabbit. Each bunny tail
       has a lower case letter on it. Pick a bunny tail. Find the rabbit with the
       capital letter that matches the lower case letter on the tail. Then tack that
       tail onto that rabbit. One by one, pin each tail onto the correct rabbit.

       Each rabbit tail has a hole in it ready for you to put the thumbtack
       through. The hole will always be at the top of the tail. This will help you
       make sure you have the letter right side up.

       You will want to work on this activity by yourself. When you have
       finished pinning the tails on the rabbits, ask (name a top student who
       thoroughly knows the letters) to come check your rabbits with you to
       make sure you have the tails on the correct rabbits.

LETTER MATCH AND STRING

PURPOSE: Matching capital and lower case letters

MATERIALS: colored railroad board
scissors
compass
permanent felt-tip markers
2 medium-sized manila envelopes
rubber cement
laminating materials
art knife
yarn

PREPARATION: Cut 2 circles out of colored railroad board. Each circle should be 14″ in diameter. Print 13 capital letters along the edge of the left half of one circle. Print the matching lower case letters in a random order along the edge of the right half of the circle. (See the illustration.) Print the other 13 capital and lower case letters along the edge of the other cardboard circle in a similar manner.

Turn each cardboard circle over. Cut the gummed flaps off 2 medium-sized manila envelopes. Glue one envelope on the back of each circle. Laminate both circles. Slit the openings of each envelope. Cut slits, approximately ¼″ long, around the edge of each cardboard circle, one slit beside each letter.

Cut 26 pieces of yarn, each 17″ long. Put 13 pieces of yarn in the envelope on the back of one cardboard circle. Put the other 13 pieces of yarn in the envelope on the back of the other cardboard circle.

PROCEDURE: The student matches capital letters with lower case letters by stringing pieces of yarn between the matching letters.

SAY: We have a new activity to add to our activity shelves. It is called Letter Match and String. There are 2 different cards. On the back of each card is an envelope containing pieces of yarn.

Select a circle to work on. Remove the pieces of yarn from the envelope on the back. Take one piece of yarn. Slide one end of the yarn into a slit beside a capital letter on the left side. Then find the lower case letter that matches that capital letter. Slide the other end of that piece of yarn into the slit by that letter.

Pick up another piece of yarn. Put one end through the slit beside a capital letter and the other end through the slit beside the matching lower case letter. Continue matching all of the capital letters with their matching lower case letters in this way.

When you are finished, bring your circle to me and together we will look over the letters to make sure you have matched them correctly. Then take the pieces of yarn out of the slits and put them back into the envelope ready for another student to use.

Remember, there are 2 different cards in the set. You will want to do the second one, too.

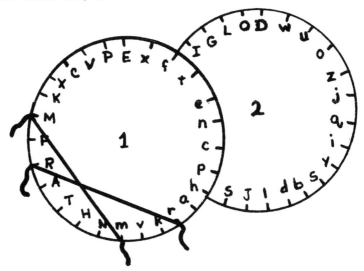

POPSICLE LETTERS

PURPOSE: Matching capital and lower case letters

MATERIALS: orange, red, and purple construction paper
 52 popsicle sticks
 scissors
 laminating materials (optional)
 rubber cement
 watercolor black felt-tip marker

PREPARATION: Cut 16 popsicle shapes out of one color of construction paper. Cut 18 popsicle shapes out of each of the other two colors of construction paper.
 Print a capital letter on one construction paper popsicle. Print the lower case letter on another popsicle of the same color. Do the same for each of the letters, printing the capital and lower case form of the letter on popsicles of the same color. Laminate the popsicles, if possible. Then glue a popsicle stick to the back of each popsicle so that it extends down from the popsicle.

PROCEDURE: Have the students put the popsicles together by matching capital with corresponding lower case letters.

SAY: Put the popsicles together by matching capital with corresponding lower case letters.

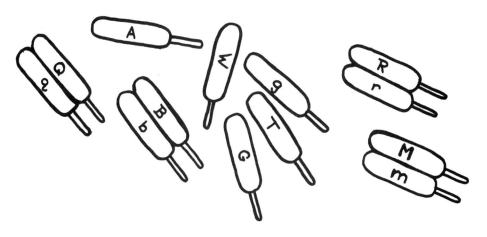

ACORN ALPHABET

PURPOSE: Matching capital and lower case letters

MATERIALS: 2 shades of brown construction paper
                     scissors
                     watercolor black felt-tip marker
                     laminating materials (optional)

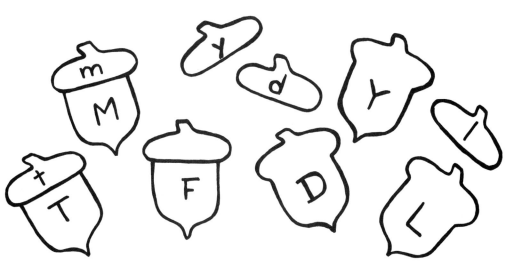

PREPARATION: Cut 26 acorns out of brown construction paper. Cut 26 acorn caps out of a darker shade of brown construction paper. Print a different lower case letter on each acorn cap. Print a different capital letter on each acorn. Laminate all pieces, if desired.

PROCEDURE: Have the students put acorn caps on the acorns by matching capital letters with corresponding lower case letters.

SAY: Put the acorn caps on the acorns by matching capital letters with the corresponding lower case letters.

*THUNDERSTORM!**

PURPOSE: Matching capital with lower case letters

MATERIALS: 14″ × 22″ sheet of blue railroad board or posterboard
construction paper of a contrasting shade of blue
yellow construction paper
scissors
rubber cement
water color felt-tip markers
manila envelope
art knife
laminating materials

PREPARATION: Draw stormy-looking rain clouds on the railroad board or posterboard. Cut out a jagged flash of lightning from the yellow construction paper. Glue this onto the railroad board. Glue a manila envelope to the back of this activity board. Tuck the flap into the envelope.

Cut out 26 large raindrops from the blue construction paper, making each raindrop a slightly different size or shape. Print a different lower case letter on each raindrop. Place the 26 raindrops on the activity board. Trace around the raindrops one at a time to make an outline of each on the activity board. Print a capital letter in each raindrop outline corresponding to the lower case letter of the raindrop that fits in that outline.

Laminate all pieces. Carefully slit open the opening to the manila envelope.

PROCEDURE: Have the student(s) place each raindrop on its activity board outline by matching lower case letters with capital letters. This activity is self-correcting. Each raindrop will fit exactly on only one outline.

---

*Indicates a self-correcting activity.

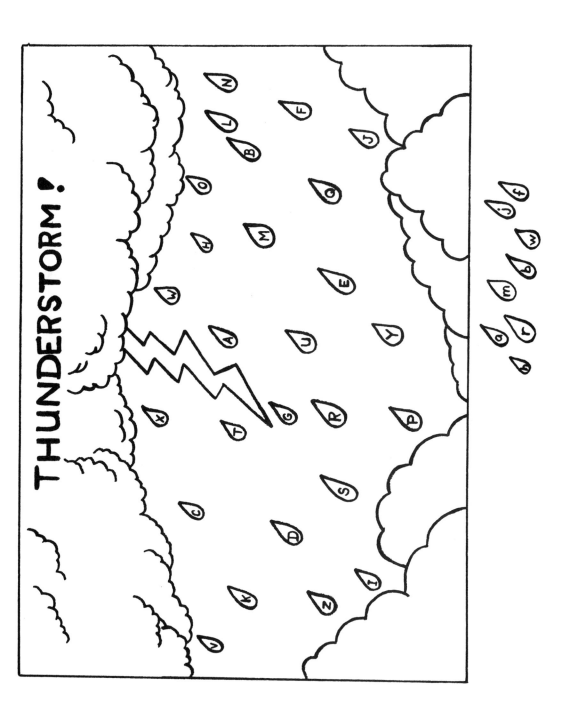

SAY: Spread all of the raindrops out, letter side up. Place each raindrop on its activity board outline by matching lower case letters with capital letters.

When you are finished with this activity, store the raindrops in the envelope on the back of the activity board.

HATCHING BIRDS

PURPOSE: Matching capital with lower case letters

MATERIALS: white tagboard or railroad board
yellow construction paper or railroad board
scissors
watercolor black felt-tip marker
laminating materials

PREPARATION: Cut 26 broken eggs out of white tagboard or railroad board. Cut 26 baby birds out of yellow construction paper or railroad board. Print a different capital letter on each broken egg. Print a different lower case letter on each baby bird. Laminate.

Note: This activity can be made self-correcting by printing, very small, the capital form of the letter on the back of each bird. When the child has completed the activity, he can then turn the birds over one at a time to see if the capital letter on the back of the bird matches the capital letter on the egg in which he placed the bird.

PROCEDURE: Have the student(s) place each baby bird back ''into'' (behind but exposed) the correct egg by matching capital letters with corresponding lower case letters.

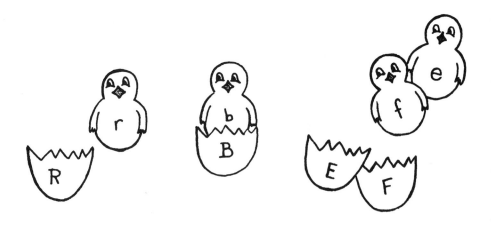

SAY: Place each baby bird back "into" (behind but exposed) the correct egg by matching capital letters with corresponding lower case letters. When you have finished, ask (name a student who thoroughly knows the letters) or me to check your baby birds to make sure you have put them into the correct shells.

A B C GUM

PURPOSE: Matching capital with lower case letters

MATERIALS: a stick of gum
green construction paper
gray railroad board or posterboard or construction paper
scissors
permanent black felt-tip marker
laminating materials
glue

PREPARATION: You will need a real stick of gum to use as a pattern. Carefully remove the outer paper wrapper and spread it out flat. Use this as a pattern, tracing around it on sheets of green construction paper to make 26 wrappers. Cut these out. Laminate. Fold each piece slightly larger than the original wrapper and glue each together so that you have 26 "gum wrappers." Print a different capital letter on each gum wrapper.

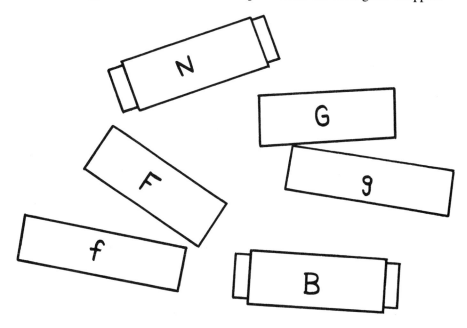

Using the piece of gum as a pattern, trace around it on gray railroad board, posterboard or construction paper to make 26 "pieces of gum." Cut these out and laminate. Print a different lower case letter on each "piece of gum."

PROCEDURE: Have the student(s) slide each piece of gum into the correct gum wrapper by matching capital with lower case letters.

SAY: Slide each piece of gum into the correct gum wrapper by matching capital letters with corresponding lower case letters.

ALPHABET SCHOOL

PURPOSE: Matching capital with lower case letters

MATERIALS: 14″ × 22″ sheet of railroad board or posterboard
art knife
felt-tip markers
oaktag or railroad board
rubber cement
scissors
manila envelope
laminating materials
transparent tape

PREPARATION: On the railroad board or posterboard, draw 26 students' desks, a teacher's desk, and any other classroom items. (See the illustration.) With an art knife, carefully cut slots approximately 1½″ long across the back of each student desk. Print a different lower case letter on each student desk.

Cut out 29 "students" from oaktag or railroad board. Add some features. Print a different capital letter on each.

On the back side of the activity board, tape strips of oaktag across the slots to form pockets into which the "students" will slide when put into the slots from the front. Glue a manila envelope onto the back side of the activity board. Tuck the flap into the envelope.

Laminate the activity board and the "students." Cut apart the slots and the opening of the envelope.

PROCEDURE: Have the student(s) slide each "student" into the slot behind the desk with the corresponding lower case letter.

SAY: Lay the activity board on a table and spread out the ''students,'' letter side up. Slide each ''student'' into the slot behind the desk with the corresponding lower case letter.

When you have finished the activity, bring it up for me to check. Then take the ''students'' out of the desk slots and store them in the envelope on the back of the board.

CAPITAL-LOWER CASE MATCH CARDS

PURPOSE: Matching capital with lower case letters

MATERIALS: 5 sheets of 9″ × 12″ colored railroad board or posterboard
permanent black felt-tip marker
yarn
scissors
bookbinding tape or plastic tape

PREPARATION: Draw a straight line vertically through the center of each card. Next, print 5 capital letters on the left side of each card in a random order. (Print 6 letters on the fifth board.) On the right side of each board print, in a random order, the lower case form of the letters found on that board. (See the illustration.)

Next, cut 26 pieces of string or yarn, each approximately 12″ long. Line up a piece of yarn on the back side of each capital letter, with approximately 1″ of yarn on the cardboard. Tape one end of each piece of yarn to the back side of the cardboard.

Using a pair of sharp scissors, make a ½″–¾″ cut beside each lower case letter along the right-hand side of the cards.

PROCEDURE: Have the student(s) match the capital letter with the lower case letter by taking the yarn from the capital letter on the left to the corresponding lower case letter on the right, and pulling the yarn into the cut beside the letter.

SAY: Match the capital letter with the lower case letter by taking the yarn from the capital letter on the left to the corresponding lower case letter on the right. Pull the yarn into the cut in the card beside the lower case letter. Do the same with each of the letters on this card and on the rest of the cards. When finished, the pieces of yarn will run from each capital letter to each corresponding lower case letter.

When you are finished, let me check your cards. Then take the yarn out of the cuts, so that the letter matching cards will be ready to be used by another student.

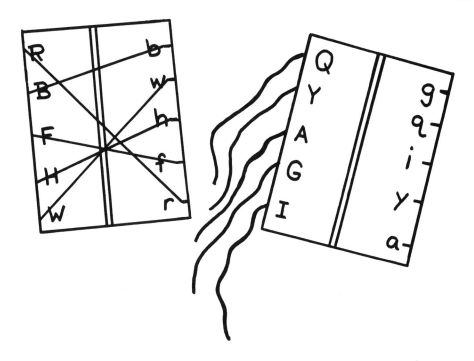

ALPHABET LION*

PURPOSE: Matching capital with lower case letters

MATERIALS: yellow railroad board or posterboard
brown or orange railroad board
pencil
permanent felt-tip markers
tracing paper
carbon paper
scissors
laminating materials (optional)

PREPARATION: On a piece of yellow railroad board or posterboard, draw a
lion as illustrated. Divide his mane into 26 sections and print a different
lower case letter in each of the sections.

Using sheets of tracing paper, trace the lion's mane and the sections
of the mane. Place the tracing paper mane and carbon paper on top of a
piece of brown or orange railroad board. Trace over the mane. Remove
the tracing paper and carbon paper. Print capital letters on the brown (or

---

*Indicates a self-correcting activity.

orange) mane in the same positions as the lower case letters on the lion. Cut out his mane and cut apart the 26 sections. Laminate, if possible.

PROCEDURE: Have the student(s) place each capital letter section of the mane on the corresponding lower case section of the lion's mane.

This activity is self-correcting. Unless a capital letter is placed on the correct lower case letter, the piece will not fit the space correctly.

SAY: Lay the yellow lion board on a table. Lay out the capital letter sections of the mane on the table letter side up. Place each capital letter section of the mane on the corresponding lower case section of the lion's mane.

If you have correctly matched the capital and lower case letters, then the sections of the lion's mane will fit together properly.

BIG EARS

PURPOSE: Matching capital and lower case letters

MATERIALS: oaktag or construction paper
colored pencils and-or washable felt-tip markers
scissors
art knife
laminating materials or clear Con-Tact paper
box

PREPARATION: Cut out 26 rabbit faces minus the ears from oaktag or construction paper. With colored pencils and/or washable felt-tip markers, draw in some rabbit features. Cut out 26 pairs of rabbit ears. Print a different capital or lower case letter on each pair of ears, one letter on each ear. Laminate the rabbit faces and ears or cover them with clear Con-Tact paper. Cut 2 slots in the top of each rabbit head so that the ears can be slid in and out of position.

Decorate a box in which to keep the rabbit faces and ears when not in use.

PROCEDURE: Have the student(s) pick out capital and lower case letter ears that go together and put those ears in the slots on a rabbit head.

SAY: In this box is an activity called Big Ears. What animal can you think of that has big ears? . . . In this box are 26 rabbits and their big ears.

To do this activity, spread all of the rabbit ears out with the letters facing up. Pick out a capital letter ear and a lower case letter ear that go

together and put those 2 ears in the slots on a rabbit head. Set that completed rabbit off to the side. Continue putting ears on each of the rabbit heads by finding the matching capital and lower case letter ears and placing them in the slots.

WHERE'S MY MOTHER?

PURPOSE: Matching capital and lower case letters

MATERIALS: white railroad board or posterboard
yellow railroad board or posterboard
black felt-tip marker
scissors
colored pencils
laminating materials or clear Con-Tact paper
Scotch Post-It Tape
sheet of paper

PREPARATION: Cut out 26 mother ducks from white railroad board or poster-board. Cut out 26 baby ducks from yellow railroad board or posterboard. Using the black felt-tip marker, print a different capital letter on each mother duck. Print a different lower case letter on each baby duck. Using colored pencils, draw in the ducks' features and color in their feet and bills. Laminate or cover with clear Con-Tact paper.

Place a long strip of Scotch Post-It Tape along a bare wall. Place the mother ducks in alphabetical order along the Post-It Tape, leaving enough space for a baby duck to be placed between two mother ducks.

Tape a blank sheet of paper on the wall beside the activity. The children will sign this sheet when they have completed the activity.

PROCEDURE: Have the student(s) help the baby ducks find their mothers by matching the lower case letter on the baby ducks with the capital letters on the mother ducks.

SAY: In my hand I have 26 baby ducks. They have lost their mothers. Along the wall are the mother ducks. Each mother duck has a capital letter printed on her. Each baby duck has a lower case letter printed on it. Can you help each baby duck find his own mother?

The baby duck with the lower case letter *a* on it belongs to the mother duck with a capital *A*. Place her baby duck behind her by pressing her baby duck onto this strip of tape. Help all of the baby ducks find their mothers in this way.

When you have finished, ask (name a top student) to check to make sure you have matched the babies with the correct mothers. Then sign your name on this sheet of paper so that I know that you have completed the activity. After that, peel the baby ducks off the tape. Then mix the baby ducks up and set them on this table ready for another student to use. Be careful not to take the mother ducks off the tape.

TONGUE DEPRESSOR LETTER MATCH-UP

PURPOSE: Matching capital and lower case letters

MATERIALS: 52 tongue depressors
permanent green felt-tip marker
permanent blue felt-tip marker
box or can
Con-Tact paper
scissors

PREPARATION: You will need 52 tongue depressors. Use the green marker to print a different capital letter on each of 26 of the tongue depressors. Use the blue marker to print a different lower case letter on each of the remaining 26 tongue depressors.

Store the tongue depressors, when not in use, in a small box or can covered with Con-Tact paper.

PROCEDURE: Have the student(s) match the capital letter sticks with the corresponding lower case letter sticks, as illustrated.

SAY: Match the capital letter sticks with the corresponding lower case letter sticks. (Demonstrate.) When you have finished the acitivity put the letter sticks back in this box ready for another student.

MAIL A LETTER

PURPOSE: Differentiating between capital and lower case letters, letter recognition and knowledge

MATERIALS: box with a lid (a hosiery box or candy box)
dark blue construction paper or railroad board
art knife
paper cutter
felt-tip markers
rubber cement
laminating materials
assorted colors of construction paper

PREPARATION: Cut a piece of dark blue construction paper or railroad board to fit on top of the box lid. As illustrated, draw and label 2 mailboxes on this blue piece. Carefully cut out the openings in the mailboxes. Laminate. Then glue this piece to the box lid. Cut through the cardboard box lid to make the mailbox openings go through the lid.

Cut a piece of construction paper 2″ longer than the width of the inside box bottom and to the same height as the box bottom. Fold this strip 1″ from each end so that one end folds in one direction and the other end folds in the other direction. Put glue on each folded end. Place this strip across the inside center of the box, gluing the ends to the sides of the box. This strip will divide the box into two compartments, one for capital letters and one for lower case letters.

Using several colors of construction paper, cut 52 small rectangles small enough to slide through the mailbox openings in the lid. Print a different capital or lower case letter on each piece and draw a miniature stamp in the upper right hand corner of each. These will be the "letters."

PROCEDURE: Have the student(s) sort the letters into the appropriate mailbox according to whether the envelope has a capital or lower case letter on it.

SAY: Sort the letters into the appropriate mailbox depending on whether the envelope has a capital or a lower case letter. When you have completed the activity, I will open the box and check it with you to make sure that all the letters in the capital letter compartment are capitals and all the letters in the lower case letter compartment are lower case.

After we have checked the letters, mix them up and put them back in the box ready for another student to sort.

*ALPHABET SOUP**

PURPOSE: Differentiating between capital and lower case letters, letter recognition and knowledge

MATERIALS: 14″ × 22″ sheet of railroad board or posterboard
permanent felt-tip markers
art knife
scissors
2 medium-sized manila envelopes
rubber cement
laminating materials or clear Con-Tact paper
bright-colored construction paper

PREPARATION: On the railroad board or posterboard, draw 2 large kettles and label them as illustrated. Carefully cut a straight slot, about 4″ long, horizontally across the top of each kettle.

---

*Indicates a self-correcting activity.

Cut the flaps off 2 medium-sized manila envelopes. Cut a 4″ slot in one side of each manila envelope. Glue each envelope to the back of the activity board, lining up the slots on the envelopes with the slots on the activity board. On the envelope glued behind the kettle for the capital letters, print Capital Letters. Then print *each* of the capital letters on that envelope. Print Lower Case Letters on the other envelope. Then print each of the lower case letters on that envelope.

Laminate both sides of the activity board or cover with clear Con-Tact paper. Then carefully cut open the slots and the top opening of each envelope.

Next, you will need to make the letter cards. Cut 52 cards, each 2″ × 2″, from bright construction paper. Print a different capital or lower case letter on each card.

PROCEDURE: Have the student(s) place each letter into the correct kettle, depending on whether it is a capital letter or a lower case letter. This activity is self-correcting. When finished sorting the letter cards into the kettles, the student turns the activity board over, removes the letter cards from one of the envelopes and checks to make sure that each of those letter cards actually belongs in that envelope by checking that each letter on the cards is listed on that envelope. The student then checks the other envelope in the same way.

SAY: We have been learning to recognize the capital and lower case letters of the alphabet. Today we have a new activity to work on the alphabet letters. This activity is called Alphabet Soup. See the two kettles of alphabet soup. This kettle says Capital Letters. And this kettle says Lower Case Letters.

Here are the alphabet letters that need to be put into the soup kettles to make the soup absolutely delicious! However, only capital letters can go into the kettle marked Capital Letters. And only lower case letters can go into the kettle marked Lower Case Letters. If you get letters into the wrong kettle, it will make the alphabet soup taste horrible!

You are to place each letter into the correct kettle, depending on whether it is a capital letter or a lower case letter.

When you have finished, turn the activity board over and you will see 2 envelopes, one marked Capital Letters and one marked Lower Case Letters. On each envelope is listed the letters that belong in that particular envelope. Reach into one envelope and pull out all the letter cards. Make sure that each of those letter cards actually belongs in that kettle of soup by checking that each letter on the cards is listed on that envelope. Check the letters in the other envelope in the same way. Then mix the letter cards up and place them in one of the envelopes ready for another person to sort.

CLIP IT

PURPOSE: Matching capital and lower case letters

MATERIALS: colorful railroad board or posterboard
scissors
felt-tip marker
laminating materials or clear Con-Tact paper
26 spring-type clothespins
box
attractive Con-Tact paper

PREPARATION: Cut an octagon out of colorful railroad board or posterboard. With a felt-tip marker, print the 26 capital letters on 7 of the 8 sides. Leave one side with no letters. (See the illustration.) Laminate or cover ·with clear Con-Tact paper.

Clip 26 spring-type clothespins onto the activity board, one over each of the 26 capital letters. Print the lower case letter that corresponds to the capital letter on each clothespin. Print all letters on the clothespins in such a way that when the clothespin is clipped onto the activity board in the correct place, the letter will be right side up.

Cover a box with decorative Con-Tact paper. Store the clothespins in this box.

PROCEDURE: Have the student(s) clip each clothespin over the capital letter that matches the lower case letter.

SAY: Here is a fun activity that will help you practice matching lower case letters with their capital letters.

On this board are all of the capital letters of the alphabet. In this box there are clothespins. Each clothespin has a different lower case letter printed on it. Pick up a clothespin, read the letter on it, find the capital letter on this board, and clip the clothespin on the board over that letter. Clip each clothespin over the capital letter that matches the lower case letter.

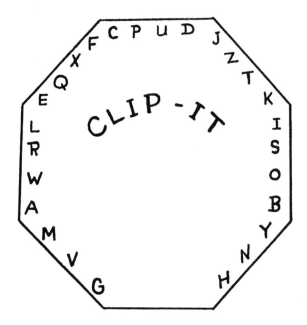

SELF-CORRECTING ALPHABET MATCHING CARDS*

PURPOSE: Matching capital and lower case letters

MATERIALS: 13 unlined blue file cards, each 3″ × 5″
13 unlined pink file cards, each 3″ × 5″
paper cutter or scissors
washable black felt-tip marker
washable red felt-tip marker
washable blue felt-tip marker
laminating materials (optional)
paper punch

---

*Indicates a self-correcting activity.

PREPARATION: Cut all the file cards in half to make 26 cards of each color. On each of the pink cards, print a different capital letter with a washable black felt-tip marker. Across the bottom of each card make a stripe with a red marker. On each of the blue cards print a different lower case letter with the black marker. Then make a blue stripe across the bottom of each blue card. Laminate, if desired.

   Place a capital letter card evenly on top of the matching lower case letter card, and punch a hole in the two letter cards with a paper punch. (See the illustration.) Do the same with the other matching pairs of letter cards, punching the holes in slightly different positions for each of the different pairs.

PROCEDURE: Have the students match the capital letters with the corresponding lower case letters. This activity is self-correcting. The students can check their accuracy by placing the capital letter card over the top of the lower case letter card. If correct, the holes in the 2 cards will line up.

 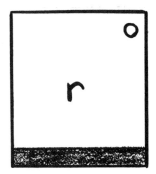

SAY: Mix the cards together. Then spread them out letter side up. The color stripe should be along the bottom edge of each card. This stripe will help you make sure you have the letters right side up. Match the capital letters with the corresponding lower case letters. Check your accuracy by placing the capital letter card over the top of the lower case letter card. If correct, the holes in the 2 cards will line up.

FIND IT—STRING IT

PURPOSE: Matching capital and lower case letters

MATERIALS: colors of railroad board
               paper cutter
               ruler
               old wallpaper sample book
               rubber cement
               felt-tip marker
               paper punch
               laminating materials or clear Con-Tact paper
               yarn
               bookbinding tape or plastic tape

PREPARATION: Cut 26 rectangles, each 4" × 2½", from various colors of railroad board. Next, you will need a wallpaper sample book. (Paint and wallpaper stores usually give away old wallpaper sample books free.) Cut 26 rectangles, each 3" × 1½", from various colors and types of lightly patterned wallpaper. Glue a different wallpaper rectangle onto each of the 26 railroad board rectangles.

     Print a different capital letter on the left side of each of the cards. On the right side of each card print various lower case letters, making sure that one of the letters on each card corresponds to the capital letter on that card. Laminate the cards or cover with clear Con-Tact paper.

     Use the paper punch to punch one hole on the right side of the capital letter. Punch one hole to the left of each lower case letter. (See the illustration.) Cut 26 pieces of yarn, each approximately 4½" long. Insert a small amount of the yarn through the hole beside the capital letter. Tape it securely on the back side of the card. Do the same with each card.

Variation: To make this a self-correcting activity, on the reverse side of each card draw a small smiling face beside the hole with the correct answer

PROCEDURE: The student selects a card, picks up the end of the piece of yarn, and sticks it through the hole beside the lower case letter that goes with the capital letter on that card. The rest of the cards are done in the same manner.

SAY: Here is a set of cards to help you practice recognizing capital letters and their matching lower case letters. (Hold up a card.) Over here you see 3 lower case letters. One of these 3 letters goes with the capital letter on this card. Pick up the end of the piece of yarn, stick it through the hole beside the lower case letter that goes with the capital letter. Pull the yarn so that a yarn line joins the 2 matching letters. Do the same with the rest of the cards.

You may do this activity by yourself or with a friend.

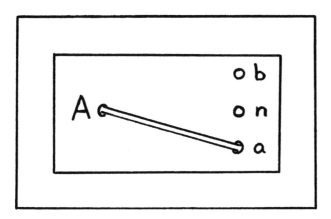

BUILD A WALL*

PURPOSE: Matching capital and lower case letters

MATERIALS: 14" × 14" sheet of railroad board
felt-tip markers
colored pencils (optional)
tracing paper
carbon paper
reddish-brown construction paper
scissors
rubber cement
small manila envelope
laminating materials or clear Con-Tact paper
art knife

*Indicates a self-correcting activity.

PREPARATION: Draw a wall on the railroad board, as illustrated. Draw the
outlines of 26 stones on the wall, making each stone a slightly different
size. Print a different capital letter in each stone outline. Draw Humpty
Dumpty sitting on the wall.

Use tracing paper and trace around each stone outline. Print on the
tracing paper stone the lower case letter that corresponds to the capital
letter on the stone outline. Place the tracing paper on top of a piece of
carbon paper on the sheet of reddish-brown construction paper. Trace
over the tracing paper stones and their letters. Cut out these stones. Go
over the letters on the stones with a felt-tip marker.

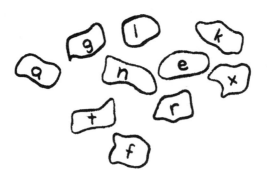

Glue a small manila envelope to the back of the activity board. Tuck in the flap on the envelope.

Laminate all parts or cover with clear Con-Tact paper. Slit open the opening in the manila envelope.

PROCEDURE: Have the students place each stone on its stone outline on the wall by matching lower case letters with corresponding capital letters.

This activity is self-correcting. Each stone is a slightly different size or shape and will fit only the outline with the corresponding capital letter.

SAY: Lay the activity board on a table. Lay out the stones letter side up. Place each stone on its stone outline on the wall by matching lower case letters with the corresponding capital letters.

If you have correctly matched the capital letters with the lower case letters, then the stones will fit exactly on the stone outlines. Correct any mistakes you may make.

Store the stones in the envelope on the back of the activity board when not in use.

PLANT THE SEEDS

PURPOSE: Matching lower case with capital letters

MATERIALS: red or orange construction paper or railroad board
tan construction paper
brown construction paper
black fine felt-tip marker
brown colored pencil
scissors
rubber cement
laminating materials
art knife

PREPARATION: Cut 26 flower pots from red or orange construction paper or railroad board. (See the illustration.) Color an area of soil brown on each flower pot. Cut a slot, approximately ½″ × 2″, in the soil of each pot. Cut 26 rectangles, approximately 2″ × 3″, from brown construction paper. Glue one of these rectangles over the slot on the back of each flower pot. Glue only around the edges of the rectangle so that a pocket is formed in the center. Print a different capital letter on the front of each flower pot.

Cut out 104 seeds from the tan construction paper. Make the seeds approximately ½″ × ¾″. Use the black marker to print the lower case letters on the seeds, printing each letter on both sides of four seeds.

Laminate both sides of the flower pots and seeds. Cut open the slot on each pot.

PROCEDURE: Have the student plant each seed in the flower pot with the corresponding capital letter by sliding the seeds into the slots in the flower pots.

        If not all the letters have been taught, use only those flower pots and seeds for letters which have been taught.

SAY: Plant each seed in the flower pot with the corresponding capital letter by sliding the seeds into the slots in the flower pots.

        When you have finished the activity, I will check to make sure you have put the seeds into the correct flower pots.

SKUNK

PURPOSE: Letter recognition and matching capital with lower case letters

MATERIALS: unlined file cards
               1 regular playing card
               scissors
               black fine felt-tip marker
               picture of a skunk
               rubber cement
               laminating materials or clear Con-Tact paper

PREPARATION: Using a regular playing card as a stencil, cut out 53 cards from unlined file cards. On each of 52 cards, print a different capital or lower case letter. Print the same letter on each end of the card so that, no matter how the cards are shuffled, when spread out in the hand the letters will be visible. (See the illustration.) On the one remaining card, glue a picture of a skunk.

Laminate the cards or cover them with clear Con-Tact paper.

PROCEDURE: This card game is played like Old Maid, as the students match capital letters with corresponding lower case letters and try not to end up with the card with the picture of the skunk.

Three or four players can play this game at a time. To play, shuffle the cards thoroughly, then deal out all of the cards face down, one at a time, to each player in a normal dealing fashion.

SAY: We are going to play an alphabet card game called SKUNK. Pick up the cards I have dealt you. Look for matching capital and lower case letter cards in the cards in your hand. If you have a matching pair, say ''I match (B) with (b),'' and lay the matching cards in a pile in the center of the table.

When you have removed all of the matching pairs of cards in this way, we will be ready to begin.

The first player draws a card from the hand of the player to his left. If it matches with one in his hand, he says, ''I match _____ with _____,'' and lays down the matching pair on the center pile. If it does not match with a card in his hand, he puts it in his hand with the rest of his cards. It is then the next player's turn to draw a card from the hand of the player on his left.

We will continue playing until all capital and lower case letters are matched and one player is left holding the card with the skunk. The player with the skunk loses. All the other players win.

ALPHABET FISH

PURPOSE: Letter recognition and matching capital with lower case letters

MATERIALS: unlined file cards
              1 regular playing card
              scissors
              fine felt-tip marker
              colored pencils (optional)
              laminating materials or clear Con-Tact paper

PREPARATION: Using a regular playing card as a stencil, cut out 52 cards
from unlined file cards. If you want a title card for the card game, cut out
one extra card and write Alphabet Fish on it. With the fine felt-tip marker,
print a different capital or lower case letter on each of the 52 cards. Print
the same letter on each end so that no matter how the cards are shuffled,
when spread out in the hand the letters will be visible. You may decorate
the cards with the colored pencils, if desired. (See the illustration.) Laminate the cards or cover with clear Con-Tact paper.

PROCEDURE: This card game is played like the regular card game of Go Fish,
except that the students are matching capital letters with corresponding
lower case letters.

   Two to four players can play this game at a time. To play, shuffle the
cards thoroughly, then deal the cards face down one at a time until each
player has 7 cards. The remaining undealt cards are placed face down in a
stack in the center of the table. These undealt cards are called the ''Fish
Pile.''

SAY: We are going to play a card game called Alphabet Fish. Pick up the cards
I have dealt you. Look for matching capital and lower case letter cards in
your hand. If you have a matching pair, show us the pair and say, ''I
match _____ with _____,'' and lay the matching cards in a pile
beside you on the table. Keep your pile of matched cards separate from
those of the other players.

   When you have removed all of the matching cards in this way, we
will be ready to begin the game.

   The first player will look over the cards in his hand, select a letter for
which he needs a matching letter card, and then ask another player if he
has that card. For example, Billy might say, ''Jimmy, do you have an
M?'' If the other player has the requested card, he must give it to the
player asking for it. The first player will then show the pair, and say, ''I
match _____ with _____,'' and put the 2 matching cards on his

pile on the table. He will then ask the same player or another player for another letter card he needs. When he asks a player for a letter card that the other player does not have, the other player tells him to "Go Fish." He will then draw a card from the "Fish Pile," the pile of cards in the center of the table. It then will become the next player's turn to ask for the letter cards he needs.

Play continues in this way until all of the capital and lower case letters are matched and none of the players have any cards left in their hands. The players then count the cards in their piles. The player with the most cards is the winner.

LETTER MATCHING
(A bulletin board activity)

PURPOSE: Matching capital and lower case letters

MATERIALS: bright-colored construction paper (2 different colors)
paper cutter
black felt-tip marker
yarn
bulletin board
26 spring-type clothespins
scissors
stapler and staples
26 thumbtacks

PREPARATION: Cut 26 identical pieces of bright-colored construction paper. Print a different capital letter on each. Then cut 26 pieces of a different color of construction paper. Print a different lower case letter on each.
Staple the capital letters in a random order onto the left third of a wall bulletin board. Cut 26 pieces of yarn. Tie a spring-type clothespin to one end of each piece of yarn. Tie the other ends of the yarn pieces around

thumbtacks. Stick the tacks into the upper left-hand corner of each capital letter card, firmly attaching the yarn to the bulletin board.

Next, staple the lower case letters to the right third of the bulletin board in a random arrangement. Staple only along the right edge of each of these letter cards. Let the left side remain unfastened.

PROCEDURE: Have the student match the capital letters with the corresponding lower case letters by clipping the clothespin to the matching lower case letter cards. The matching letters will then be connected by yarn.

When the student has completed the activity, you should look over the bulletin board to make sure that the student has matched the letters correctly. Then the student should unclip the clothespins so the activity will be ready for another student to do.

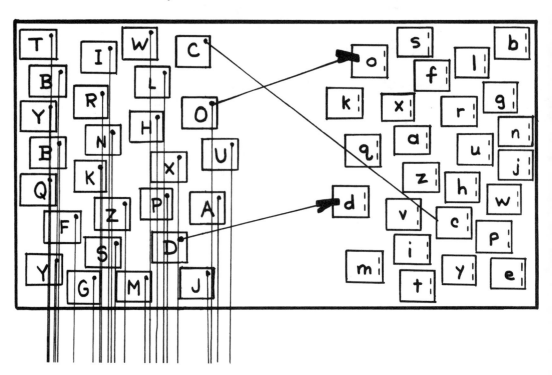

4

GAMES AND ACTIVITIES TO REINFORCE LETTER SOUND RELATIONSHIPS

SOUND CLUES IN LETTERS

PURPOSE: Letter sound relationships

MATERIALS: None

PREPARATION: None

PROCEDURE: When introducing the sound of b, d, f, j, k, l, m, n, p, r, s, t, v, or z, point out to the students that you can hear the sound of the letters when saying the letter name.

SAY: Our new letter for today is the letter (S). Watch while I print the capital letter (S) and the lower case (s) on the chalkboard. The letter (s) has the sound of (ssss). You can hear the sound of the letter (s) when you say (s). Let's say the letter (s) together and as we say it, let's listen for the (ssss) sound . . .

Let's think of some words that begin with the letter (s). I will print the words we think of on the chalkboard.

LETTER SOUND PICTURE CARD FILE

PURPOSE: Letter sound relationships

MATERIALS: shoe box and lid
attractive Con-Tact paper
3″ × 5″ alphabetical file card dividers
packs of white unlined 3″ × 5″ file cards
pictures from old workbooks, catalogs, etc.
scissors
rubber cement
laminating materials (optional)

PREPARATION: Cover a shoe box and lid with attractive Con-Tact paper. You will need a number of packs of white unlined 3″ × 5″ file cards. (Sometimes you can get unlined heavy white 3″ × 5″ cards free from a printing company's scrap pile.)

Cut out as large a number of different pictures for each initial letter sound as possible. Pictures can be cut out of old workbooks, catalogs, etc. Glue a different picture on each file card. Laminate, if desired. File the cards in the shoebox in alphabetical order by first letter. File the cards between appropriate letter file dividers.

Variation: You can also print the picture name on the back of each card. Then the students can use the word side of the cards to increase their word recognition.

PROCEDURE: When teaching the sound of a letter, remove the picture cards that begin with that sound from the file. Use these picture cards as part of your instructional materials.

SAY: Our new letter for today is the letter (M). Watch as I print the capital (M) and the lower case (m) on the chalkboard. The letter (m) makes the sound (mmmm) as in the word (monkey). (When appropriate: You can hear the sound the letter (m) makes when you say the letter name. Say (m). Do you hear the (mmmm) sound when you say the letter (m)?)

Here are some cards that have pictures of objects that begin with the sound of the letter (m). Let's say the names of these pictures and as we do, listen for the (m) sound at the beginning of each word . . .

Now I am going to hide the picture cards behind my back. Who can remember some of the pictures that begin with the sound of (m)?

PAINT A LETTER SOUND POSTER

PURPOSE: Letter sound relationships

MATERIALS: heavy white art paper, one for each student
paintbrushes
several colors of tempera paint
fine felt-tip marker
permanent wide felt-tip marker (optional)

PREPARATION: Select a letter to be used in the activity. Print the capital and lower case form of the letter on each sheet of paper with either tempera paint or permanent wide felt-tip marker.

PROCEDURE: Distribute a sheet of paper to each student. Have them paint pictures of objects that begin with the sound of the letter. As the students finish painting the pictures, use the fine marker to print the word each picture represents under each picture.

SAY: Who remembers the name of the letter on this paper? . . . It is the letter (B). Let's think of some words that begin with the sound of this letter.

Now I'm going to give you each a sheet of white paper. I want you to paint pictures of things that begin with this sound on the paper to make a poster. You will want to paint as many different pictures on your paper as you can. But each picture name must begin with the sound of our letter. You may use picture dictionaries to help you think of more words.

When you have finished painting all of your pictures, bring your letter sound poster to me. I will print the word for each picture under each picture with my pen.

BRING AND BRAG

PURPOSE: Letter 'sound relationships

MATERIALS: None

PREPARATION: None

PROCEDURE: Introduce a letter and its sound thoroughly, then instruct the students to find objects whose names begin with the sound of the letter at home that evening. Tell them to bring the objects to school the next day to share with the rest of the class.

SAY: We have been learning the letter (N) and the sound that letter makes. When you go home after school, I want you to walk slowly through each room in your house looking for objects whose names begin with the sound of our new letter, the letter (N). Take a sack along with you. Each time you find an object that begins with our letter, put it in your sack. If the object is too big to put in your sack, ask your mother or father to print its name on a piece of paper. Then you draw a picture of the object beside its name. Add that piece of paper to the collection in your sack.

Have one of your parents look through the things in your sack to make sure you don't have any things in the sack that they don't want you to have. Then bring that sack to school tomorrow. During class tomorrow, each of you will get a turn to stand up and show the rest of the class what you found that begins with the sound of the letter (N).

You will take your bags back home with you after school tomorrow.

PAPER PLATE LETTER-SOUND HUNT

PURPOSE: Letter sound relationships

MATERIALS: paper plates, one for each student
permanent felt-tip marker
old workbooks, catalogs, and magazines
scissors
white school glue

PREPARATION: Select the letter being learned by the group. Print the capital and lower case form of the letter on the center of each paper plate. Have a stack of old workbooks, catalogs, and magazines from which the students can cut pictures. The students will need scissors and white school glue.

PROCEDURE: Have the students cut out pictures of objects that begin with the sound of the specified letter and glue those pictures around the edges of their paper plates. (See the illustration.)

SAY: We have just been talking about the letter (L) and the sound that it makes. Who can name some words that begin with the sound of the letter (L)?

Now I am going to give each of you a paper plate. On the center of each paper plate is printed the capital and lower case form of the letter (L). On the table you see a stack of magazines, workbooks, and catalogs that you can cut up. I want you to look through these and cut out pictures of objects that begin with the sound of (L). Glue the pictures around the edge of the paper plate. Since the paper plate is not very large, you will want to cut out pictures that are rather small.

PICK-A-PICTURE

PURPOSE: Letter sound relationships

MATERIALS: old workbooks, catalogs, magazines or duplicator exercise pages
scissors
decorated container
sheets of paper, one for each student
pencils or crayons

PREPARATION: Cut out pictures of objects from old workbooks and catalogs or from extra duplicator exercise pages. Cut out ten pictures for each child in the group. The pictures should be pictures of objects that begin with a consonant sound. Place all of the pictures in a decorated container.

You will also need a sheet of paper and a pencil or crayon for each student.

PROCEDURE: Have the students, one at a time without looking, pick out 10 pictures. Each student then glues his ten pictures onto his papers and neatly prints beside each picture the capital and lower case form of the letter with which the name of each picture begins.

SAY: In this container are lots of pictures. (Shake the container as you talk to mix up the pictures.) I want you, one at a time without looking, to pick out 10 of the pictures. When you have your 10 pictures, take a piece of paper from the pile. Glue your 10 pictures onto your paper. Then, with a crayon or pencil, neatly print beside each picture the capital and lower case form of the letter with which the name of the picture begins. (Demonstrate.)

LETTER SOUND PLACE MATS

PURPOSE: Letter sound relationships

MATERIALS: $10'' \times 16''$ sheet of construction paper, one for each student
old magazines, catalogs and workbooks
permanent felt-tip marker
scissors
white school glue
laminating materials or clear Con-Tact paper (optional)

PREPARATION: Print a capital letter and lower case letter in the center of each sheet of construction paper.

You will also need old magazines, catalogs and workbooks, in addition to scissors, white school glue and laminating materials or clear Con-Tact paper (optional).

PROCEDURE: Distribute a sheet of construction paper to each child. Review the sound the selected letter makes. Then have the students cut out from the old magazines, catalogs, and workbooks small pictures of objects that begin with the specified sound. Have the students glue the pictures onto the construction paper. When they are finished, the students can take these home and use them as place mats.

These letter sound place mats can be laminated or covered with clear Con-Tact paper before they are sent home, in which case they can be used again and again!

SAY: Today we are going to make letter sound place mats. How many of you use place mats at home? Would you like to have your own special place mat like this? (Hold up a sample place mat you have made.)

Yesterday we talked about the letter (S). Can anyone remember what sound that letter makes? Let's think of some more words that begin with that sound.

I am going to distribute a piece of paper to each of you. You are going to turn it into a place mat. What letter is on the place mat? It is the letter (S), the letter we have just been talking about.

Beside me are some old workbooks, catalogs, and magazines. I want each of you to get a couple of these. Look through them and find pictures of objects that begin with the sound of (S). Cut the pictures out carefully and glue them onto your place mat paper.

When you are all finished, bring your letter sound place mat up for me to check. When school is over this afternoon, you may take it home. This evening you can use it as a place mat when you have dinner.

FOLD-A-PAPER (I)

PURPOSE: Letter sound relationships - initial consonant sounds

MATERIALS: sheets of paper, one for each student
watercolor felt-tip marker
old workbooks, magazines, and catalogs
white school glue

PREPARATION: Fold a sheet of paper in half horizontally and crease. Then fold the paper in thirds vertically and crease. Unfold. Select a consonant letter. Print the letter in each of the rectangles resulting from the folds. (See the illustration.)

You will need a paper like this for each student in the group. You may prepare the paper before class or you may have the students fold the paper and prepare it themselves.

You will also need a stack of old workbooks, magazines, and catalogs.

PROCEDURE: Have each student find and cut out six different pictures of objects that begin with the sound of the letter written on the papers. The students then glue one picture in each block.

Variation: Have the children draw 6 different pictures of objects that begin with the sound of the specified letter.

SAY: I am giving each of you a sheet of paper. See how the creases in the paper divide it into 6 boxes? There is a letter printed in each box. What is that letter? . . . What are some words that begin with that letter?

Here is a stack of magazines, old workbooks, and catalogs. Each of you will need to take one. Look through the magazine to find pictures of objects that begin with the letter (P). When you find a picture of an object whose name begins with the letter (P), cut it out and glue it into one of the blocks on your paper. You will need to find 6 different pictures of objects that begin with that letter sound. Glue one in each block.

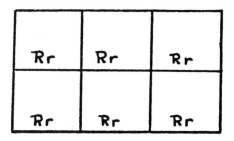

FOLD-A-PAPER (II)

PURPOSE: Letter sound relationships - initial consonant sounds

MATERIALS: sheets of paper, one for each student
watercolor felt-tip marker
old workbooks, magazines, and catalogs
scissors
white school glue

PREPARATION: Fold a sheet of paper in half horizontally and crease. Then fold the paper in thirds vertically and crease. Unfold. Select 6 different consonants. Print the capital and lower case letters of a different consonant in each block. (See the illustration.) You will need one of these for each student.

PROCEDURE: Have the students look through the old magazines, etc. to find pictures of objects whose names begin with one of the 6 letters printed on the paper. The students cut out one picture for each letter on the paper and glue each picture in the appropriate block on the paper.

Variation: Have the children draw the pictures of objects that begin with the sounds of the specified letters.

SAY: I am giving each of you a sheet of paper. It has been divided into 6 boxes by folds in the paper. There is a different letter in each box.

Here is a stack of old workbooks, magazines and catalogs.

Each of you will need to take one. Search through them for pictures of objects whose names begin with one of these 6 letters. When you find an appropriate picture, cut it out and glue it in to the correct box on your paper. You will need to find one picture for each letter.

Rr	Bb	Ss
Mm	Tt	Ff

SOUND AND SORT CUPS

PURPOSE: Letter sound relationships

MATERIALS: 6 solid-colored plastic disposable cups
permanent wide felt-tip marker
tagboard
old workbooks
rubber cement
scissors
paper cutter
colored pencils
laminating materials (optional)

PREPARATION: Select 6 letters upon which you wish the students to have reinforcing drill. Print a different letter on each of the cups. Cut a number of 1½″ × 2½″ cards from tagboard. From old workbooks, cut a number of pictures of objects that represent the initial sound of the selected letters. Glue a different picture on each card.

If you wish to make this activity self-correcting, separate the cards into piles according to beginning sound. On the back upper right-hand corner of each card beginning with the same letter, make a dot with a red colored pencil. On the back upper right-hand corner of all cards beginning with another specified letter, make a dot with a green colored pencil. Place different color dots on each of the remaining 4 sets of cards.

Laminate the picture cards, if possible.

PROCEDURE: Have the student(s) sort the cards into the appropriate letter cups according to the initial sound of the object pictured on the cards. When the student has sorted all of the picture cards into the letter cups, he can check to see that they are sorted correctly by turning over the cards in each cup and checking to see that all cards from a cup have a dot of the same color in the upper right-hand corner.

When this activity is not in use, stack the cups and place the picture cards in the top cup.

SAY: Today I want to show you our Sound and Sort Cups. Here are 6 cups. Each cup has a different letter printed on it. Each letter is a letter for which we have learned the sound in the last couple of weeks. These Sound and Sort Cups will help you practice recognizing those letter sounds.

Here is a set of picture cards. Each of these pictures begins with one of the letters on the cups. You are to look at each picture card, decide with what letter it begins, then place it in the cup with that letter printed on it.

When you have sorted all of the picture cards into the letter cups, you can check the cards yourself to see if you have sorted them correctly. Take the cards out of one cup. Turn the cards over. If they all have a dot of the same color in the upper right-hand corner, each of those cards belonged in that cup. If there are some cards with dots of other colors in that cup, you have not sorted the cards correctly. Try to figure out your mistake. If you cannot figure out your mistake, ask me to help you.

Check the cards in the other cups in the same way. All cards that belong in the same cup will have the same color dots on the back.

When you have finished the activity, stack the cups. Mix the cards thoroughly and put them in the top cup. Then put the set back on the activity table ready for another student to use.

FIND-A-PICTURE CONTEST

PURPOSE: Letter sound relationships

MATERIALS: large sheets of paper, one for each student
felt-tip marker
old workbooks, magazines and catalogs
scissors
white school glue

PREPARATION: Print the letters A–Z on each sheet of paper, leaving plenty of space between each letter. You will also need old workbooks, magazines and catalogs, and scissors and white school glue for each student.

PROCEDURE: This is a contest. The students search through magazines and cut out a picture of an object for the beginning sound of each letter of the alphabet omitting the letter x. Every student who finds a picture for the beginning sound of each letter (excluding x) of the alphabet will be considered a winner.

SAY: I am going to give each of you a piece of paper with the letters A–Z printed on it. You will need a pair of scissors and a bottle of glue. You will also need to get an old workbook, magazine, or catalog from the pile.

We are going to have a contest! Every student who finds a picture for the beginning sound of each letter of the alphabet will be considered a winner! You may omit a picture for the letter x.

Open the magazine, catalog, or workbook you have picked. Cut out a small picture of an object that begins with the short sound of *A*. Glue the picture beside the letter *A* on your paper. Next, cut out a picture of an object that begins with the sound of *B*. Glue the picture beside the letter *B* on your paper. Do the same for the rest of the letters of the alphabet. You do not need to do the letters in order. When you can't find any more pictures you can use in the magazine you are looking through, put it back on the table and get another magazine.

When you finish, bring your paper to me to look over. If you have correctly found a picture for each letter of the alphabet with the exception of x, we will write your name on a *Winners List* on the chalkboard.

TARGET PRACTICE

PURPOSE: Letter sound relationships

MATERIALS: large cardboard box
art knife
felt-tip marker
tempera paint
2 bricks
3 beanbags

PREPARATION: Cut holes in a large cardboard box to make target holes through which beanbags can be thrown. Decorate the target side of the box with tempera paint. Print a different letter under each hole. (See the illustration.) Set the target box on a table away from windows. Place 2 bricks inside the box so that it will not be toppled when hit with a beanbag.

PROCEDURE: The students line up one behind the other and take turns throwing the beanbags at the target. Each student gets 3 beanbags when it is his turn. He tries to throw them at the holes in the target. When a student throws a beanbag through a hole, he names the letter under the hole and names a word that begins with the sound of that letter. The student receives one point for each beanbag that he succeeds in throwing through a hole.

This activity works best with a small group of 1–6 students.

SAY: Today we are going to have some target practice! How many of you have tried to throw beanbags through holes in a target like this before?

We are going to line up one behind the other and take turns throwing the beanbags at our target. Each of you will get 3 beanbags when it is your turn. Throw each of them, one at a time, at the holes in the target. Try to throw each beanbag into one of the holes. You will receive one point for each beanbag that you put through a hole. When you throw a beanbag through a hole, name the letter under the hole and name a word that begins with the sound of that letter.

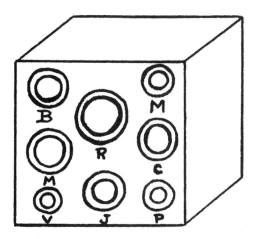

PAPER BAG SORT

PURPOSE: Letter sound relationships - initial consonants

MATERIALS: 3 small paper lunch bags
felt-tip marker
old workbooks, catalogs
scissors
rubber cement
oaktag
paper cutter
laminating materials

PREPARATION: Select 3 initial consonants upon which you wish the group to have further drill. Print a different selected letter on each side of each bag, one letter to a bag.

Use the paper cutter to cut up the oaktag into small cards. From old workbooks, catalogs and magazines, cut out a number of pictures of objects whose names begin with the selected initial consonants. Glue the pictures onto the oaktag cards. Laminate the cards.

PROCEDURE: The students take turns picking up the cards, naming the object pictured, and dropping the card into the bag showing the beginning letter for that picture.

This activity should be used with a small group of 2–10 students under teacher supervision.

Variation: Students can work on this activity independently and individually.

SAY: Children, we have been learning the sounds of the letters (b), (d), and (t). Who can tell me some words that begin with (b)? . . . Who can remember some words that begin with (d)? Good. And who can remember some words that begin with the letter (t)? You certainly have very good memories!

Today we have a new game to give us more practice on these 3 letters. Here are 3 paper bags. One bag has the letter (b) on it. One bag has the letter (d) on it. And the third bag has the letter (t) on it.

Here is a set of picture cards that begin with the sound of (b), (d) or (t). We are going to take turns picking up cards, naming the object pictured, and dropping the card into the bag showing the beginning letter for that picture.

SORT AND MATCH BOX

PURPOSE: Letter sound relationships

MATERIALS: shoe box with lid
attractive Con-Tact paper
unlined file cards
small toy objects that begin with the sounds of the selected letters
felt-tip marker

PREPARATION: Select 2–6 letters on which you wish the students to have further practice in the area of letter sound relationships. The letters selected must be ones on which you have provided thorough instruction, and which the children have mastered fairly well.

Print each selected letter on a separate file card. Cover a shoe box with Con-Tact paper. Place the letter cards in the box. Collect a number of small toy objects that begin with the sounds of the selected letters. Put the objects in the shoe box.

PROCEDURE: The student spreads the letter cards out on the table letter side up. The student then takes the objects out of the box one at a time, decides with which letter each object begins, and places the object with that letter card.

SAY: Here is a Sort and Match Box. In this box are (4) cards with the letters (f), (k), (l), and (t) printed on them. There are also a number of small toys in the box.

Place the letter cards on the table. Then take the objects out of the box one at a time. Decide with which letter each object begins and place the object with that letter card. When you have finished placing each object with the correct letter card, I will check your work. Then you may put the objects and the cards back in the box ready for another student to use.

You will want to work on this activity by yourself.

GUESS WHAT LETTER I HAVE

PURPOSE: Letter recognition and letter sound relationships

MATERIALS: 26 unlined file cards
felt-tip marker

PREPARATION: Print a different letter of the alphabet on each of 26 unlined filed cards.

PROCEDURE: Use this activity with a group of 3–8 students.

This activity is a guessing game. Shuffle the cards; then turn the letter cards so that the letters are facing down and deal one letter card to each student.

Instruct each player to peek at the letter on his or her card, but not to let anyone else see what letter is on his or her card. Each student then takes a turn standing up and letting the rest of the group guess what letter he or she has.

SAY: We are going to play a guessing game. Each of the cards I have in my hand has a different letter printed on it. I am going to mix up the letter cards, turn the letter cards so that the letters are facing down, and give you each a letter card.

Peek at the letter on your card, but don't let anyone else see what letter is on your card. You will take turns standing up and letting the rest of the group guess what letter you have.

SOUND CLOUDS*

PURPOSE: Letter sound relationships and matching capital and lower case letters

MATERIALS: white oaktag or white railroad board
scissors
blue colored pencil
gray colored pencil
black fine felt-tip marker
old workbooks
rubber cement
laminating materials or clear Con-Tact paper
box
washable transparency marking pen
paper towel

PREPARATION: From white oaktag or railroad board, cut a number of cloud shapes. These clouds can be identical or can vary somewhat in shape. Using blue and gray color pencils, shade in a few areas on the clouds to make them more cloud-like.

Select letters upon which you wish the students to have reinforcing drill. From old workbooks cut pictures of objects that begin with the various letters selected. Glue one picture on each cloud. Using the fine marker, print a combination of capital and lower case letters beneath the picture on each cloud. Be certain to include on each cloud the capital and lower case letter that goes with the picture on that cloud. (See the illustration.)

To make the clouds self-correcting, print the correct capital and lower case letter on the back side of each card.

Laminate each card or cover with clear Con-Tact paper. Decorate a box in which to keep the clouds.

You will also need a washable transparency marking pen to place in the box with the clouds.

---

*Indicates a self-correcting activity.

PROCEDURE: The student is to look at the picture at the top of a Sound Cloud
and decide with what letter its name begins. Using the washable transparency marking pen, the student is to put a circle around that capital and
lower case letter.

   This activity is self-correcting. When the student has finished all of
the Sound Clouds in this manner, he can check his answers with those on
the back of the clouds. The student then wipes off his answers with a
paper towel.

SAY: Here is a set of activity cards that will give you practice on the sounds the
various letters make. These cards are called Sound Clouds. They are
shaped like clouds.

   At the top of each Sound Cloud is a picture. Below it are a number of
letters. You are to look at the picture and decide with what letter its name
begins. Then, using this special marker, put a circle around that capital
and lower case letter. (Demonstrate.)

   When you have finished marking all of the Sound Clouds, you can
check your own answers. On the back of each cloud are the answers for
that cloud. But don't peek at the answers until *after* you have marked your
answers on the card.

   When you have finished all of the cards and checked your answers,
wipe your answers off with a paper towel. Then put the Sound Clouds and
the special pencil back in the box and put the box back on the activity
table.

TRY A TRIANGLE

PURPOSE: Letter sound relationships - initial consonants

MATERIALS: colored construction paper
             paper cutter
             scissors
             old workbooks

rubber cement
felt-tip marker
laminating materials
washable transparency marking pen
box
paper towels

PREPARATION: Use the paper cutter to cut $2'' \times 2'' \times 2''$ equilateral triangles out of colored construction paper. Cut out small picutres of objects from old workbooks. Be sure to have at least one picture representing each initial consonant sound. Glue the pictures onto the triangles, as illustrated. Draw a line under each picture. Laminate.

   You will also need a washable transparency marking pen and a box in which to keep the triangles and the pen.

PROCEDURE: Have the student pick a triangle, say the picture name to himself, think what letter he hears at the beginning of that picture name, then print that letter on the line under the picture using the washable transparency marking pen. The student does each of the triangles in this way.

SAY: Here are some triangles. Each triangle has a picture and a line underneath the picture. And here is a special pen for you to use to mark on each triangle. Pick a triangle, say the picture name to yourself, think what letter you hear at the beginning of that picture name, then print that letter on the line under the picture using the special marker. Do each of the triangles in this way.

   When you have finished, I will check your triangles. Then take a paper towel and carefully wipe off your answers. Put the triangles in this box ready for another student to use.

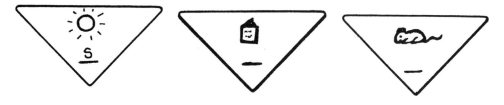

WHICH PICTURE PUZZLE ARROWS*

PURPOSE: Letter sound relationships

MATERIALS: railroad board (assorted)
                      scissors

---

*Indicates a self-correcting activity.

fine felt-tip marker
old workbooks
rubber cement
wide felt-tip marker
laminating materials or clear Con-Tact paper
washable transparency marking pen
box
paper towels

PREPARATION: Cut 20–30 arrow shapes, as illustrated, out of various colors of railroad board. Select letters upon which you want the students to drill. Using the fine marker, print one letter near the point of each arrow. From an old workbook, cut out 1–3 pictures of objects that begin with the sound of the letter printed on the first arrow. Cut out several pictures that begin with other sounds. Glue three pictures, one beneath the other, along the end of the arrow opposite the point. Turn the arrow card over and, using the wide marker, put a color dot directly behind each picture on that card that begins with the letter on that card.

   Prepare each of the remaining arrow cards using the same procedure. On each card glue 3 pictures, including 0–3 pictures of objects that begin with the sound of the letter on that card. Laminate all cards or cover with clear Con-Tact paper.

   Decorate a box in which to store the activity cards and the marker when not in use.

PROCEDURE: On each arrow-shaped card there is a letter. The student looks at the letter, thinks what sound that letter makes, then uses the washable transparency marking pen to draw a circle around each picture that begins with that letter.

   This activity is self-correcting. When he has completed all the arrows in this manner, the student can turn the arrow cards over to check his answers.

SAY: Today I am going to place a new set of activity cards on our shelves. The activity cards are called Which Picture Puzzle Arrows. You can see that each card is in the shape of an arrow.

   On each arrow-shaped card there is a letter near the point. Look at that letter, think what sound that letter makes, then use this special marking pen to draw a circle around each picture that begins with that letter. Some cards may have 1 or 2 pictures that begin with the letter on the card. Some cards may have no pictures that begin with that letter. And, on some cards all of the pictures may begin with that letter.

Whenever you have some extra time, you may get this set of activity cards to do. When you have finished marking them, you can check your own answers by checking to see where the dots are on the back side of the card. Each picture that begins with the letter on the card will have a dot behind that picture.

After you have finished checking your answers, take a paper towel and wipe off your answers. Put the arrow cards and special pen back in the box. And put the box back on the shelf ready for another student to use.

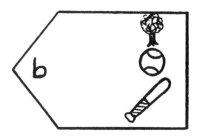

WHICH ONE DOESN'T BELONG?

PURPOSE: Letter sound relationships

MATERIALS: colored tagboard or railroad board
paper cutter
scissors
old workbooks
rubber cement
fine felt-tip marker
laminating materials or clear Con-Tact paper
box
attractive Con-Tact paper
washable transparency marking pen
paper towels

PREPARATION: Cut a number of cards 3½″ × 4″ out of colored tagboard or railroad board. Cut out pictures of objects from old workbooks that begin with various initial consonants. Glue one picture on each card. Underneath each picture, print 2 consonants, one that is the initial consonant of the pictured object, one that is not. (See the illustration.) Laminate the cards or cover with clear Con-Tact paper. Decorate a box in which to keep the cards and the transparency marking pen when not in use.

PROCEDURE: The student decides which letter is *not* the letter with which the object pictured on the card begins. He then puts an X over that letter to cross it out.

SAY: Here is a set of activity cards you may choose to work on when you have some spare time. They are called Which One Doesn't Belong?

On each card is a picture of an object and beneath the picture are 2 letters. You are to decide which letter is *not* the letter with which the name of that object begins. Then put an X over that letter to cross it out. Use this special pen to cross out the letter that doesn't belong.

You will work on these cards by yourself. When you have finished marking them, bring them up for me to check. Then you can wipe your answers off with a paper towel and put the cards back ready for another student to do.

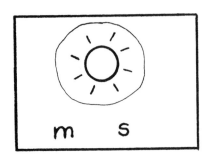   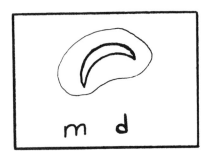

*CROSS IT OUT ACTIVITY CARDS**

PURPOSE: Letter sound relationships—initial consonants

MATERIALS: various colors of railroad board
compass
scissors
felt-tip marker
old workbooks and catalogs
rubber cement
Laminating materials or clear Con-Tact paper
3–4 washable transparency marking pens
paper towels

PREPARATION: Use the compass to draw 4″ × 8″ half moon shapes on various colors of railroad board. Cut out the shapes. Print a different consonant on

*Indicates a self-correcting activity.

each piece. From old workbooks and catalogs, cut out a number of small pictures, most of which begin with the selected consonants. On each activity board glue a number of pictures, most of which begin with the consonant printed on that board, a few that begin with other consonants. (See the illustration.) On the back of each board, put a tiny X behind each picture that does not begin with the consonant printed on that card. Laminate each card or cover with clear Con-Tact paper.

You will also need several washable transparency marking pens.

PROCEDURE: Using the washable transparency marking pen, the student puts an X on each picture that does not begin with the consonant printed on the card. This activity is self-correcting. When he has completed a card, the student turns the card over to check his answers.

SAY: Today we have a new set of activity cards. They are called Cross It Out Activity Cards. These cards will help you practice recognizing the letter sound at the beginning of various words.

Each card has a letter printed on it and then a number of pictures around the edge. You are to look at the letter on the card and think of the sound it makes. Then look at the pictures on the card and use this special marking pen to cross out any picture that doesn't begin with that letter sound.

When you have finished, turn the card over. On the back of the card you will find a tiny X behind each picture that should have been crossed out. If you did not cross out a picture that has an X behind it, or if you crossed out too many pictures, look at each of those answers again and try to determine why your answer is incorrect.

When you have finished a card and checked your answers, wipe your answers off with a paper towel. Then place the card on the activity table and get another card to do.

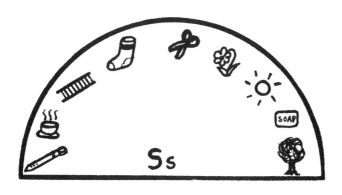

SOUND-SHAPE ACTIVITY CARDS

PURPOSE: Letter sound relationships

MATERIALS: assorted colors of railroad board or posterboard
scissors
permanent felt-tip markers
workbooks
laminating materials or clear Con-Tact paper
rubber cement
3–4 washable transparency marking pens
paper towels

PREPARATION: Select letters upon which you wish the students to practice. Decide upon an object shape you wish to represent the initial consonant sound of each of your selected letters. Cut each object shape out of colored railroad board or posterboard. (See the illustration.) Print the letter at the top of the shape. These Sound-Shape Cards should be approximately 9″ × 12″, varying according to the individual object represented.

Find workbook pages of exercises for each of the letters selected. Glue one page of exercises on each activity card, matching the letter drilled in the exercise with the letter represented by the Sound-Shape Card. Laminate each card or cover with clear Con-Tact paper.

PROCEDURE: Have the student fill in the exercise on the Sound-Shape Card using the transparency marking pen. The teacher checks the answers on the activity card. Then the student wipes the answers off the activity card with a paper towel.

SAY: We have been learning the sounds of the various letters. Here is a new set of activity cards that will give you practice recognizing the various letter sounds at the beginning of words. These cards are called Sound-Shape Activity Cards.

Select a Sound-Shape Activity Card and a special marking pen. On the card you will find an exercise that works on the letter for that card. You are to mark your answers right on the activity card using a special marking pen. If you forget the sound of the letter on your activity card, the shape of your activity card will give you a clue to the sound the letter makes. For example, the card for the letter (h) is in the shape of a (hat). The sound you hear at the beginning of (hat) is the sound of the letter (h).

When you have completed marking the answers on your card, let me check it with you. Then wipe off your answers with a paper towel and put the activity card and the special marking pen back ready for someone else to use.

You may do the activity cards, one by one, as you have time.

NAME THAT SOUND ACTIVITY CARDS

PURPOSE: Letter sound relationships—initial consonants

MATERIALS: children's magazines or old reading books
scissors
rubber cement
10 sheets of 9″ × 12″ oaktag
ruler
black fine felt-tip marker
laminating materials
6–10 washable transparency marking pens
paper towels

PREPARATION: Cut 10 full-page color pictures out of children's magazines or old reading books. Trim the pictures down to 6½″ × 9″ or smaller. Glue each picture onto a separate sheet of oaktag. Draw straight lines from some of the objects in the pictures to the closest edge of the picture and extend ½″ onto the oaktag. (See the illustration.)
Laminate the cards.

PROCEDURE: The student selects a card and notes the black lines drawn from some of the objects to the edge of the card. Using one of the marking pens, he prints along the edge of the card at the end of the line the letter with which each object begins.

SAY: Here is a set of activity cards called Name That Sound Activity Cards. There are 10 cards, each with a different picture. Let's look at one of the cards. Do you see the black lines drawn from some of the objects to the edge of the card? Using one of these special marking pens, you are to print along the edge of the card at the end of the line the letter with which the object begins.

I would like each of you to take a card and a special pen. Fill in the letters for your card. When you have finished your card, hand it to me to check. When I have checked it and all of your answers are correct, take a paper towel and wipe off all your answers. Then trade cards with someone else who is also done and do the new card.

SOUNDS IN THE WINDOW*
(File folder activity cards)

PURPOSE: Letter sound relationships

MATERIALS: several file folders
ruler
scissors
old workbooks and catalogs
rubber cement

---

*Indicates a self-correcting activity.

fine felt-tip pen
laminating materials
3–5 washable transparency marking pens
paper towels
oaktag
paper cutter

PREPARATION: Cut out a rectangular window on the front of each file folder. Print a different number in the upper right-hand corner of each file folder.

From old workbooks and catalogs, cut out a number of small pictures of objects that begin with letter sounds upon which you wish the students to drill. Glue the pictures on the inside right-hand side of the file folder. Glue the pictures in rows, leaving at least at 1½" border of no pictures around the four sides. Draw a line approximately ¾" long under each picture.

Laminate each file folder in an open position. Then fold each file folder closed and crease.

To make answer keys for the activity cards, cut oaktag to the exact size of the file folder. Mark the same number in the upper right-hand corner of the answer card as appears on the activity card. Then print the answers, spaced as on the activity cards.

PROCEDURE: The students will print the letters for the objects pictured on the plastic window with the markers.

This activity is self-correcting. To check answers, the answer card that has the corresponding number on it is placed inside the file folder with the edges of the answer card lined up with the edges of the activity card. The plastic window is then folded over the answer key so the correct answers on the answer key show through the plastic near or underneath the student's answers.

SAY: Boys and girls, today we have a new set of activity cards. They are called Sounds in the Window. There is a plastic window on each activity card. Underneath each plastic window are pictures and lines under each picture. With one of these special marking pens, you are to print on the plastic window the letter with which each picture begins. Print the letters on the lines under the pictures. (Demonstrate.)

When you have finished marking your answers on your Sounds in the Window Card, get the answer key for your card. In the upper right-hand corner of your activity card is a number. Select the answer card that has the same number on it. Place the answer key inside the file folder, carefully lining up the edges of the answer key with the edges of the activity card. Fold the plastic window over the answer key and check your answers. The correct answers on the answer key will show through the plastic near or underneath your answers. (Demonstrate.)

Put a circle around any incorrect answers. Then remove the answer key and try to correct your mistakes by looking again at the pictures.

When you have finished, wipe your answers off with a paper towel and put the activity card, the answer key, and the special pen back for another student to use.

You will want to do each of the cards during the next week.

ROUND AND AROUND ALPHABET GAME

PURPOSE: Letter sound relationships

MATERIALS: colored railroad board or posterboard
               compass
               permanent black felt-tip marker
               laminating materials or clear Con-Tact paper
               scissors
               paper fastener
               paper clip
               game markers

PREPARATION: Cut out a round game board, approximately 22″ in diameter, from colorful railroad board or posterboard. Cut out another circle 3″ in diameter to make a spinner.

Draw a spiraling game path, as illustrated. Print *Start* in the center and *Win* in the last outside space. Print a letter in each space along the path. Laminate or cover with clear Con-Tact paper.

To make the spinner, divide the small cardboard circle into 3 pie-shaped sections. Write a numeral in each section. Laminate. Then punch a hole through the center of the circle. Insert a paper fastener through a paper clip, then through the hole in the center. Bend the prongs of the paper fastener, leaving it somewhat loose so that the paper clip will spin easily.

You will also need several game markers.

PROCEDURE: Players place markers on *Start* and take turns spinning the spinner and moving forward the number of spaces indicated. Each player must name the letter on the space on which he lands and name a word that begins with that letter. If he cannot, someone else must help him and he must move his marker back one space.

SAY: Today I am going to let 3 of you play a new letter sound game. Tomorrow three other people can play the game. The game is called Round and Around Alphabet Game, round because the game board is round and around because you go around and around the game board.

To play the game, each player chooses a marker and places his marker on the center section that says *Start*. The first player spins the spinner and moves his marker forward the number of spaces indicated on the spinner. He must then name the letter on the space on which he landed and name a word that begins with that letter. If he cannot, someone else must help him and then he must move his marker back one space. It is then the next player's turn to spin the spinner, move his marker forward, etc.

Play continues in this way. The winner is the first player to reach *Win*. However, the player must spin the exact number needed to move onto *Win*. If he spins a number too large, he cannot move his marker. He must wait until it is his turn again and try to spin a number that he can use to move onto *Win*.

A STARRY NIGHT

PURPOSE: Letter sound relationships—initial consonants

MATERIALS: 14″ × 22″ sheet of blue railroad board or posterboard
yellow railroad board or construction paper
black felt-tip marker
old workbooks and catalogs
scissors
rubber cement
laminating materials

PREPARATION: Cut 14–20 stars of identical size and shape from the yellow
railroad board or construction paper. Use one of those stars as a pattern to
draw the outlines of 14–20 stars on the blue railroad board or posterboard.
Draw the same number of outlines of stars as stars you have cut out. (See
the illustration.) Outline the stars on the blue railroad board. Select which
letter sounds you want to use on the activity board. Print one letter in each
star outline on the activity board.

Cut out small pictures of objects from old workbooks and catalogs that begin with the consonants selected for the activity board. You will need one picture to correspond to each letter used in the stars on the activity board. Glue one picture onto each yellow star. Laminate the activity board and the stars.

PROCEDURE: The student spreads the stars out on the table, picture side up. The student then picks up a star, decides with what letter sound the object in the picture begins, then places that star on the activity board outline that has that letter printed on it. The student follows the same procedure with the rest of the stars.

This is an activity for students to work on individually or in pairs.

SAY: This activity is called A Starry Night. On this activity board are the outlines of a number of stars. A letter is printed in each star outline. And here are the stars that fit in the outlines on the activity board. Each star has a picture on it. Spread the stars out on the table, picture side up. Pick up a star, decide with what letter sound the object in the picture begins, then place that star on the activity board outline that has that letter printed in it. Follow the same procedure with the rest of the stars.

LETTER SHAPE-SOUND CARDS

PURPOSE: Letter sound relationships—initial consonants

MATERIALS: assorted colors of railroad board or posterboard
scissors
felt-tip markers
old workbooks or catalogs
rubber cement
laminating materials
yarn
bookbinding tape or strong plastic tape

PREPARATION: For some or all of the consonants except X, cut out an object shape from the railroad board or posterboard to represent the initial consonant sound of that letter. Each card should be approximately 9″ × 12″, varying somewhat according to the individual object represented. (See the illustration.)

Print the appropriate capital and lower case letters on each individual shape card. From old workbooks or catalogs, cut out a number of small pictures representing the initial consonant sounds of each of the letters. Around the edges of each card, glue a number of pictures of objects representing the initial consonant sound of that letter. Also glue on several pictures of objects that begin with other initial consonant sounds.

Cut a little notch in the cardboard above or beside each picture. Laminate each card and cut the notches again.

Cut a number of pieces of yarn. Count the number of pictures on a card that represent the initial consonant sound of that particular letter. Then attach that number of pieces of yarn to the card by taping one end of each piece of yarn to the back side of the card behind the letter. Do the same with each of the other cards.

PROCEDURE: The student strings pieces of yarn from the letter on the Letter Shape-Sound Card to the pictures that go with that beginning sound.

SAY: Here is a set of activity cards you will enjoy doing. These cards will help you practice recognizing words that begin with certain letters.

Select a card. Think what letter is on the card and what sound that letter makes. The shape of the card will give you a clue as to the sound that letter makes. For example, the card for the letter (F) is in the shape of a (fish). The sound you hear at the beginning of (fish) is the sound of the letter (F).

Look at each of the pictures on your card. Decide which pictures begin with the sound of the letter on your card. String pieces of yarn from the letter to the pictures that go with that beginning sound. Insert the yarn through the notches of the correct pictures.

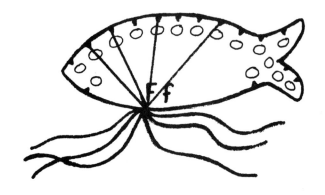

HELP THE FLOWERS BLOOM
(A flannel board activity)

PURPOSE: Letter sound relationships

MATERIALS: yellow railroad board
compass scissors
velour paper
6 different colors of railroad board (excluding yellow)
rubber cement
old workbooks
felt-tip marker
flannel board

PREPARATION: Cut 6 circles, 2″ in diameter, out of yellow railroad board. Cut out sets of eight flower petals from 6 different colors of railroad board. Glue pieces of velour paper to the back of each circle. Print a different consonant letter in the center of each of the 6 circles. Glue a piece of velour paper to the back of each flower petal. For each of the 6 consonants, cut out 8 different small pictures of objects from old workbooks whose names begin with that consonant. Glue a picture on each petal. Pictures should be glued onto petals of random colors, so that *not*

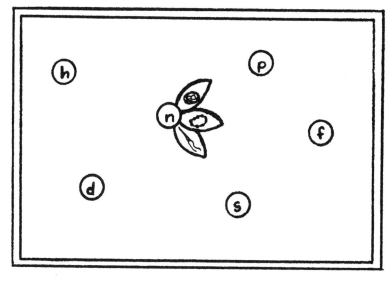

all pictures with the same initial consonant sound end up on petals of the same color.

You will also need a flannel board.

PROCEDURE: Put the flower centers on the flannel board. Have the student spread out the petals picture side up. The student then picks up a petal, notices the picture on it, thinks of the beginning sound of the picture, and places that petal near the flower center that has that letter printed on it. (See the illustration.) The student does the same with each of the petals, making 6 flowers.

SAY: On the flannel board are the centers of six flowers. Here are the petals to turn these centers into beautiful flowers. Each of the petals has a picture on it. Spread out the petals with the picture side up. Pick up a petal, notice the picture on it, and think of the beginning sound of the picture. Think what letter makes that sound. Then place that petal near the flower center that has that letter printed on it. It will stick to the flannel board.

Do the same with each of the petals. When you have finished, you will have created 6 beautiful flowers and you will have practiced your beginning sounds. Let me know when you have finished so that I can come check your flowers with you.

You will want to work on this activity by yourself. You may take turns.

HAPPY FACE—SAD FACE

PURPOSE: Letter sound relationships

MATERIALS: None

PREPARATION: None

PROCEDURE: The teacher names a word and then names a letter that may or may not be the letter with which that word begins. If the word begins with the sound of the letter the teacher names, the students smile and show a happy face. If the word does not begin with the sound of the letter the teacher names, the students give the teacher a very sad look.

This activity has the advantage of providing drill while not stigmatizing students for incorrect answers. Only the teacher will know which students are giving incorrect responses.

During this activity, make a mental note of those children responding incorrectly and provide further instruction for them in the near future. Do not scold students for incorrect responses or otherwise bring students responding incorrectly to the attention of other students in the class. But do let the whole group know what the correct response should have been after each word-letter problem.

SAY: We have a new game to play today. It is called Happy Face-Sad Face. Let me see you all make a very happy face. Now let me see you make a very, very sad face:

I am going to name a word. Then I am going to name a letter that may or may not be the letter with which that word begins. If the word begins with the sound of the letter I named, smile and show me a happy face. If the word does not begin with the sound of the letter I named, give me a very sad look—sad, as if you are very sad because I don't know the right one.

A B C GAME

PURPOSE: Letter sound relationships

MATERIALS: colored railroad board or posterboard
yardstick
scissors
permanent felt-tip markers
unlined file cards
paper cutter
old workbooks and catalogs
rubber cement
laminating materials (optional)
die
game markers

PREPARATION: From the colored railroad board or posterboard, cut an equilateral triangle with sides approximately 16″ long. Round off the corners. Draw a game board as illustrated. Cut a number of unlined file cards to approximately 1½″ × 2½″. From old workbooks and catalogs, cut a number of small pictures of objects representing the initial consonant sounds of various letters upon which you wish the students to drill. Glue a different picture on each card. Laminate the game board and cards, if possible.

PROCEDURE: Shuffle the cards and set them on the game board with the pictures facing down. Players place their markers on START and take turns drawing a card, naming the object pictured, telling the letter with which that object begins, throwing the die and moving the marker forward the number of spaces indicated by the die.

SAY: Today I am going to show you a new game that will give you practice recognizing the beginning sound of various words. The name of the game is A B C Game. Two or three people can play this game at one time.

To play the game, shuffle the cards and then set them on the game board with the pictures facing down. Place your markers on *Start*. The first player draws a card, names the object pictured, and tells the letter with which that object begins. If he is correct, he may throw the die and move his marker forward that number of spaces. If he is not correct, he loses his turn. If both players are not sure if he is correct, have them ask another student who you are sure would know. It is then the next player's turn to draw a card, name the object, name the letter with which it begins, throw the die and move his marker forward. Play continues in this way. The first player to reach *Win* is the *Winner*.

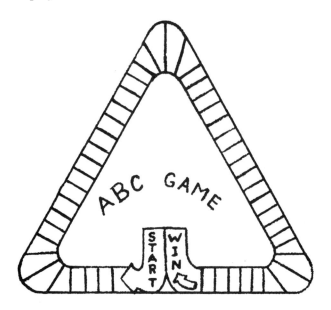

SOUND·BALLOONS

PURPOSE: Letter sound relationships

MATERIALS: 18″ × 18″ sheet of railroad board or posterboard
compass
yarn or string

scissors
white school glue
fine felt-tip markers
assorted bright-colored construction paper
old workbooks and catalogs
rubber cement
manila envelope
laminating materials or clear Con-Tact paper
art knife

PREPARATION: On the railroad board or posterboard, draw round balloons, all of the same size. With white school glue, glue small pieces of yarn or string from the end of each balloon, making the balloons look as though they had gotten loose and were blowing away in the wind. (See the illustration.)

Select consonants upon which you wish the students to drill. Out of old workbooks and catalogs, cut small pictures of objects whose names have the selected consonants in the initial position. With rubber cement, glue one picture on each balloon.

Out of bright colors of construction paper, cut circles the size of the balloons on the activity board. You will need one circle for each balloon on the activity board. Print on each circle one of the selected consonants to correspond with each activity board balloon picture.

Cut the flap off a manila envelope and glue the envelope to the back of the activity board.

Laminate the activity board and the letter balloons or cover with clear Con-Tact paper. Slit open the opening to the manila envelope. Store the letter balloons in this envelope when the activity board is not in use.

PROCEDURE: The student matches the letter balloon to the picture that begins with that letter, and places the letter balloon on top of the activity board balloon to which it corresponds.

SAY: We have been learning the sounds that the different letters make. Today I am going to show you a new activity that will help you practice recognizing those letter sounds. The activity is called Sound Balloons.

Here is the activity board. On it are the outlines of balloons. In the balloon outlines there are pictures. In the envelope on the back of the activity board are the colored letter balloons. Each letter balloon has a letter printed on it. Spread the letter baloons out with the letter side up. Look at the picture in a balloon outline on the activity board. Decide with what letter that picture begins. Find a letter balloon that has that letter printed on it. Place that letter balloon on top of the activity board balloon.

Continue placing letter balloons on top of the activity board balloon outlines, matching the letter to the picture that begins with that letter.

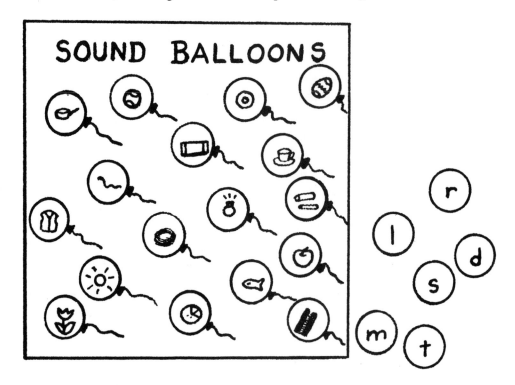

ALPHABET PIGGY BANKS

PURPOSE: Letter sound relationships and alphabetical order

MATERIALS: old wallpaper sample book
                scissors
                art knife
                16″ × 22″ sheet of colored railroad board (other than yellow)
                felt-tip markers
                5 small manila envelopes
                rubber cement
                compass
                yellow oaktag or railroad board
                laminating materials or clear Con-Tact paper
                old workbooks

PREPARATION: Obtain an old wallpaper sample book from a wallpaper
dealer. (You can usually get outdated wallpaper sample books free just by
asking.)

Cut 5 piggy bank shapes out of wallpaper samples, each one out of a
different wallpaper pattern. Glue the piggy banks onto the sheet of colored railroad board. (See the illustration.) Carefully cut out a 2" × ¼" slot
in each pig. "Coins" will be slipped into these slots. Mark each bank
with letters.

Cut the flaps off 5 small manila envelopes. Cut a 2" × ¼" slot in one
side of each envelope, as illustrated.

Glue each envelope to the back of the activity board, lining the slots
on the envelopes up with the slots on the activity board. On the envelope
glued behind the piggy bank with the letters A–E, print the letters A–E.
Print letters that correspond with the other banks on the other four envelopes.

Laminate both sides of the activity board or cover with clear Con-
Tact paper. Then carefully cut open the slots and the top opening of each
envelope.

To make the coins, draw circles 1¼" in diameter on the yellow
oaktag or railroad board. Cut these out. From old workbooks, cut a
number of small pictures of objects representing the initial sounds of the
various letters. If desired, cut out more than one picture for each letter.
Omit pictures for the letter X. Glue a different picture on each coin.
Laminate the coins.

This activity can be used as a teacher-directed activity with a small
group of students, as a learning center activity, or as an activity students
can work on independently and individually in their spare time.

PROCEDURE: The students take turns picking up coins, naming the picture on
the coin, naming the letter with which the picture begins, and sliding the
coin into the bank in which it belongs.

SAY: (For teacher-directed small group activity) Today we are going to play a
piggy bank game. How many banks do we have on our game board? Look
at the letters on the piggy banks. The first piggy bank has the letters A–E
printed on it.

Here are the coins. Each coin has a different picture on it. Only coins
with pictures whose names begin with the letters A, B, C, D, or E can be
slid into the first piggy bank. (Etc.)

Let's spread all of the coins out on the table with the picture side up.
We will take turns picking up coins, naming the picture on the coin,

naming the letter with which the picture begins, and sliding the coin into the bank in which it belongs.

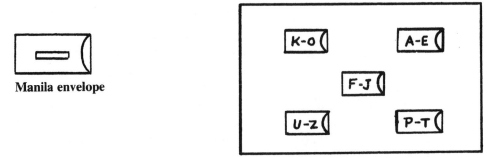

Manila envelope

Back of activity board

UP THE MOUNTAIN!

PURPOSE: Letter sound relationships

MATERIALS: 14″ × 22″ sheet of railroad board or posterboard
felt-tip markers
yarn
2 large colorful buttons
bookbinding tape or strong plastic tape
scissors

PREPARATION: On the railroad board or posterboard, draw a mountain as illustrated. Print letters going up each side of the mountain. Punch a hole near the top of one side of the mountain and at the bottom of the same side of the mountain. Put a piece of yarn through one of the holes and tape it onto the backside of the cardboard. String a large colorful button onto the yarn. Then put the other end of the piece of yarn through the other hole and tape it onto the back side of the cardboard. Follow the same procedure on the other side of the mountain.

PROCEDURE: This activity can be used by two students at a time. The students take turns moving their buttons up the mountain one letter at a time. As a student moves his button to the next letter, he must correctly name that letter. If he cannot name the letter correctly, the teacher tells him the

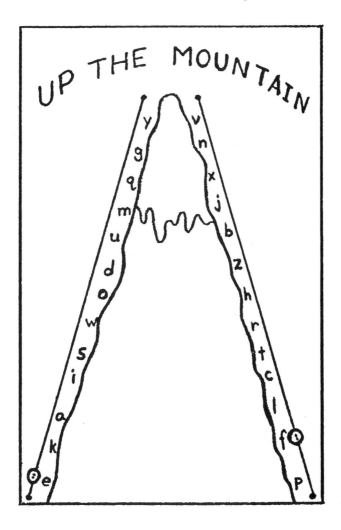

name of the letter. The student must then move his button down a letter. It is then the other player's turn.

SAY: Today you are going to climb a mountain. Have you ever climbed a mountain before? . . . This is the mountain we are going to climb. Do you see the letters of the alphabet going up each side of the mountain?

You will need to choose which side of the mountain you are going to climb. You will take turns moving your button up the mountain, one letter at a time. When you move your button up to the next letter, you must correctly name the letter. If you cannot name the letter correctly, I will tell you the letter name, but you must move your button one letter back down the mountain. When it is your turn again, you can move your button back onto that letter and try to name the letter again.

The first player to reach the top of the mountain with his button is the champion mountain climber.

GO FLY A KITE
(A bulletin board activity)

PURPOSE: Letter sound relationships

MATERIALS: light blue paper
     white paper
     bulletin board
     stapler & staples
     push pins.
     assorted colors of construction paper
     paper punch
     scissors
     old workbooks
     rubber cement
     washable felt-tip marker
     laminating materials (optional)
     colored yarn
     white school glue
     thumbtacks
     chair

PREPARATION: Cover a bulletin board with light blue paper. Cut out some large clouds from white paper and staple them to the bulletin board. Pin letters across the top of the bulletin board to make the title Go Fly a Kite.

From construction paper, cut out a number of kites, approximately 4″ × 7″. Punch a hole in the top side of each kite. Cut pictures from old workbooks to represent the initial letter sounds upon which you wish the group to drill. Using rubber cement, glue one picture on each kite. On the back of each kite, use the washable felt-tip marker to print the initial letter of the object pictured on the reverse side. Laminate kites, if desired.

Cut pieces of colored yarn approximately 5″ long to use as tails on the kites. Cut rectangles approximately ¼″ × ½″ from colored construction paper. Using big blobs of white school glue, glue the pieces of construction paper at intervals along each yarn kite tail. Glue one end of each tail securely to the back side of each kite.

PROCEDURE: This is a teacher-directed small group activity.

The students take turns picking up a kite, naming the picture on the kite and naming the letter with which that picture begins. The students then tack their kites up on the bulletin board.

VARIATION:* When the students have finished ''flying kites'' as a group activity, they can be instructed to do it in their spare time as an independent activity, either individually or in pairs. The students should lay the kites down, picture side up. They should pick up the kites, one by one, think to themselves or say aloud the beginning letter of the object pictured on the kite, turn the kite over and compare their answer to the letter printed on the reverse side of the kite, then tack the kite up in the sky.

SAY: Today we are going to fly some kites. How many of you have flown a kite before? . . . There are our kites. The bulletin board is our sky.

We are going to make the kites fly by taking turns tacking them on our sky. Here is a chair you may climb upon if you want to tack your kite up really high.

We will start with (Stephanie). (Stephanie), pick up a kite. Tell us what picture is on your kite and tell us the letter with which that picture begins. Then take a thumbtack and tack your kite up anywhere on the sky. Be sure to put the tack through the little hole in the kite.

*HOT DOG!**

PURPOSE: Letter sound relationships

---

*Indicates a self-correcting activity.

MATERIALS: reddish-brown construction paper
             oaktag or light tan construction paper
             scissors
             old workbooks and catalogs
             rubber cement
             watercolor felt-tip markers
             laminating materials
             stapler and staples
             box or manila envelope

PREPARATION: Out of reddish-brown construction paper, cut 30 hot dogs. Out of oaktag or light tan construction paper, cut 30 hot dog buns in an open position.

Select 4–20 consonants (do not include X) upon which you wish the students to drill. Out of old workbooks and catalogs, cut 30 small pictures whose names have the selected consonants in the initial position. Glue one picture on each hot dog. On the reverse side of the hot dog, in the upper right-hand corner, print the initial consonant of the picture. Print the letter *very* small.

Print on one side of each hot dog bun one of the selected consonants to correspond with each hot dog picture. Be sure to print each letter so that when the bun is folded the letter will be right side up.

Laminate all hot dogs and hot dog buns. Fold each bun through the center so that the hot dogs can be placed in the buns in the usual manner. Crease buns along the fold. Staple each bun approximately ⅓″ in from the fold in two places parallel to the fold.

Decorate a box or a manila envelope in which to keep the hot dogs and buns when not in use.

PROCEDURE: The student places the hot dogs in the buns by matching the letter with which the name of the object pictured on a hot dog begins with the letter on the bun that corresponds to that sound.

This activity is self-correcting. When finished, the student checks his accuracy by turning over each hot dog and checking to see if the tiny letter printed on the back right side of each hot dog is the same letter as is on the bun in which the student placed the hot dog.

Variation: This activity can be made into a game with each player selecting an even number of hot dogs. Buns are placed letter side down. Students take turns drawing hot dog buns and trying to match them with their hot dogs. If the hot dog bun drawn by a player does not match any of his hot dogs, he must put it back, letter side down on the table, and wait for another turn. The first player to find buns for each of his hot dogs is the winner.

SAY: Boys and girls, today we have a new activity to add to our center on beginning sounds. This activity is called Hot Dog! You can do it by yourself or with a friend. You will like this activity so well you will want to do it several times!

First, spread all of the hot dogs out on a table or desk, picture side up. Then spread out the hot dog buns, letter side up. Now pick up a hot dog, decide with what letter the object on the hot dog begins, find a bun that has that letter printed on it, and slide that hot dog into the bun. (Demonstrate.) Continue putting the hot dogs into the correct buns in this manner.

When you have finished, you can check to make sure you have put each hot dog into the correct bun. Turn the hot dog in the bun over. On the back right side of each hot dog you will see a tiny letter printed. That letter is the letter with which the object pictured on the other side begins. If that letter is the same letter as on the bun, you have placed the hot dog in the right bun.

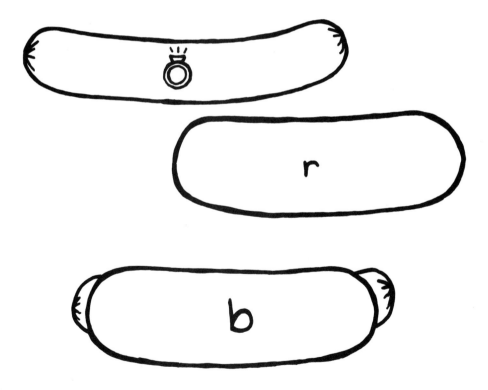

If you have placed any hot dogs in the wrong buns, look again at the picture on that hot dog, decide with what letter it really begins, then place it in the correct bun.

BEAUTIFUL TURTLE

PURPOSE: Letter sound relationships—initial consonants

MATERIALS: 14″ × 22″ sheet of railroad board
permanent black felt-tip marker
old workbook or catalog
rubber cement
tracing paper
carbon paper
assorted bright colors of construction paper or railroad board
scissors
manila envelope
art knife
laminating materials

PREPARATION: On the railroad board, outline a large turtle. Divide his shell into sections large enough for a small picture to be glued in each section. Select 5–10 consonants on which you wish the group to drill. Cut out several pictures from an old workbook or catalog to represent the initial consonant sounds chosen. Glue a different picture on each space on the turtle's shell.

Next, trace each section of the turtle's shell onto tracing paper. Using tracing paper and carbon paper, trace the sections of the shell onto a variety of bright colors of construction paper or railroad board. Fit each section of the shell on the cardboard outline of that shell section. On each cutout shell section print the initial consonant that goes with the object pictured on the cardboard outline of that shell section.

Glue a manila envelope to the back of the cardboard. Laminate the activity board and each of the cutout shell sections.

Slit open the opening to the manila envelope. Store the shell pieces in this envelope when the activity board is not in use.

PROCEDURE: This activity can be used with a group of 2–8 students under teacher supervision.

The students take turns putting the shell pieces on the turtle by matching the consonant to the picture whose name begins with that sound.

Variation: This game board can be used instead as an activity board with students working on the activity independently and individually. The activity is self-correcting since only the section of shell that belongs on an outline will fit that outline.

SAY: The last few days we have been learning the sounds of the letters (b), (f), (l), (m) and (t). Today I have a game to help us practice those letter sounds some more. The game is called Beautiful Turtle.

In the envelope on the back of the game board are the turtle's beautiful pieces of shell. We will spread out the shell pieces, letter side up.

Now look at the turtle on the game board. What is the picture in this section? That's right, it is a (fish). What letter sound do you hear at the beginning of (fish)? Yes, it is the letter (f). Now look at the pieces of shell and find one that has that letter on it and will fit this outline. If we pick up a shell piece that has the right letter on it but is the wrong shape to fit the outline, we put it back and find another piece of shell that has the right letter and will fit the outline.

We will take turns putting the shell pieces on the turtle in this manner. When we have placed all of the pieces of shell on our turtle, he will truly be the most beautiful and colorful turtle you have ever seen.

FILL THE NESTS

PURPOSE: Letter sound relationships

MATERIALS: 14″ × 22″ sheet of railroad board
             felt-tip markers
             colored pencils
             art knife

oaktag or construction paper
scissors
old workbooks
rubber cement
laminating materials

PREPARATION: On the railroad board, draw and color in a tree and birds' nests similar to that illustrated. Print the game title, Fill the Nests, at the top of the board. Make 5–8 slits in each nest. Select 7 consonant sounds to be practiced in this activity. Print a different letter on each nest. Cut 5–8 birds' eggs for each nest out of construction paper or oaktag. From old workbooks, cut out 5–8 different small pictures of objects for each of the selected initial consonants. Glue each picture onto a different egg. Laminate the eggs and the activity board. Cut open the slits in the nests.

PROCEDURE: The students place each egg in its correct nest by matching the beginning sound of the pictures on the eggs with the corresponding letters on the nests and sliding the eggs into the slots of the correct nests.

SAY: Here is a new activity you will enjoy. In my hand are some birds' eggs. On each egg is a picture. There are 7 nests in the tree. Each nest has a letter printed on it. You are to place each egg in its correct nest by matching the beginning sound of the pictures on the eggs with the corresponding letters on the nests and sliding the eggs into the slots of the correct nests.

CRAZY HOOK*

PURPOSE: Letter sound relationships—initial consonant sounds

MATERIALS: colored railroad board or posterboard
scissors
permanent black wide felt-tip marker
oaktag or unlined file cards
old workbooks
paper cutter
rubber cement
fine felt-tip marker
laminating materials
game markers
die

*Indicates a self-correcting activity.

PREPARATION: Out of colored railroad board or posterboard, cut a large hook-shaped object, as illustrated. Using a permanent black wide felt-tip marker, draw lines to divide the hook into sections. Mark *Start* at the top of the hook. Mark *Win* at the end of the inner curve of the hook.

Cut 2″ × 3″ cards from oaktag or unlined file cards. From an old workbook, cut pictures of objects that begin with initial consonant sounds upon which you wish your students to drill. Glue one picture to each card. On the back of each card, in tiny print, print the initial consonant of the picture on that card.

Laminate the cards and the Crazy Hook game board.

You will also need 3–4 markers for the game and a die.

PROCEDURE: This game can be played by 2–4 players. The first player picks up the top card, says the name of the object pictured on the card, and names the letter with which it begins. He then turns the card over. On the back of the card is printed the letter with which the picture on that card begins. If the letter on the card is the same as the letter he named, he may throw the die and move his marker forward that number of spaces. If the letter on the back of the card is not the same as the letter he named, he was incorrect and cannot throw the die and move his marker. It is then the next player's turn. Play continues in this way.

SAY: We have been learning the letter sounds we hear at the beginning of many, many words. Today we have a new game to help us practice recognizing those letter sounds.

The name of the game is Crazy Hook. Isn't this the craziest looking fishhook you have ever seen? See how it keeps on curving around!

To play the game, set the game board on the table. Each player chooses a marker and places his marker on *Start* at the top of the hook. Then shuffle the cards and set them in a pile, picture side up.

The first player picks up the top card, says the name of the object pictured on the card, and names the letter with which it begins. He then turns the card over. On the back of the card is printed the letter with which the picture on that card begins. If the letter on the card is the same as the letter he named, he may throw the die and move his marker forward that number of spaces. If the letter on the back of the card is not the same as the letter he said, he was incorrect and cannot throw the die and move his marker.

It is then the next player's turn to take a card, name the object and name the letter with which it begins, turn the card over and check his answer, then throw the die and move his marker forward.

Play continues in this way. The winner is the first player to land on *Win*. However, to move your marker on to *Win* you must throw the exact number needed. If you are only 2 spaces from *Win* and you throw the number 3 on the die, you cannot move onto *Win* because the number is too big. You would have to leave your marker where it is and wait until your next turn to try again.

There are 2 rules that are very important. Rule #1 is you *must* take the card on top when it is your turn. Rule #2 is you *must not* look at the letter on the back of the card until you have named aloud the letter with which the picture begins.

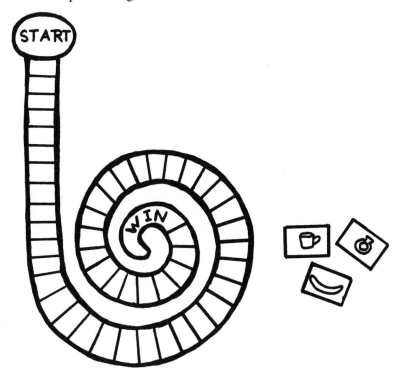

SPIN AND MOVE

PURPOSE: Letter sound relationships

MATERIALS: 18″ × 20″ piece of solid colored oilcloth or vinyl
assorted colors of permanent felt-tip markers
compass
scissors

railroad board
paper fastener
paper clip
masking tape
game markers

PREPARATION: Draw a colorful game board on the oilcloth or vinyl, as illustrated. Select 4–6 letters upon which you wish the students to have reinforcing drill. Print those selected letters in the spaces on the game board.

To make a spinner, cut a circle with a 4″ diameter out of railroad board. Punch a hole in the center of the circle. Insert a paper fastener through a paper clip, then through the hole in the circle. Bend the prongs of the paper fastener, leaving the paper fastener loose enough so that the paper clip will spin easily. Put a piece of masking tape across the prongs of the paper fastener, taping them onto the back of the cardboard spinner. Draw 4–6 lines on the front of the spinner to form equal sized, pie-shaped sections. Divide the spinner into as many sections as there are different letters on the game board. Print one letter in each spinner section. The letters on the spinner should be the same letters as on the game board.

You will also need game markers.

PROCEDURE: Two to four students can play this game at a time. The first player spins the spinner, names the letter to which the spinner points, names a word that begins with that letter, then moves his marker forward to the first space that contains that letter. It is then the next player's turn.

Note: This game board can be rolled or folded up for easy storage.

SAY: Here is a new game called Spin and Move. Playing this game will give you practice on the letter sounds we have been learning.

Two, three, or four people can play this game at a time. Each player chooses a marker and places it on *Begin*. The first player spins the spinner, names the letter to which the spinner points, names a word that begins with that letter, then moves his marker forward to the first space that contains that letter. It is then the next player's turn to spin.

Play continues in this way until a player moves onto the last letter space. When he lands there, he slides automatically into *Win* and becomes the *winner* of the game.

Any player who, on his turn, is unable to name the letter to which the spinner points or name a word that begins with that letter, loses his turn without moving his marker.

Each player is required to give a different word than has already been given in the game.

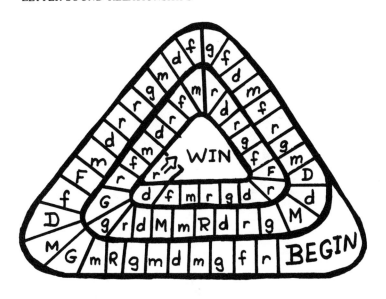

THE WITCH'S MAGIC BREWS

PURPOSE: Letter sound relationships

MATERIALS: 14″ × 22″ sheet of railroad board or posterboard
permanent black felt-tip marker
art knife
scissors
3 medium-sized manila envelopes
rubber cement
laminating materials or clear Con-Tact paper
oaktag or unlined file cards
paper cutter
old workbooks

PREPARATION: Draw 3 bubbling witch cauldrons on the railroad board or posterboard. Select 3 consonants upon which you wish the students to have reinforcing drill. Print a different consonant on each cauldron. Then carefully cut a straight slot about 3″ × ¼″ in the bubbling brew of each cauldron. (See illustration.)

Cut the flaps off 3 medium-sized manila envelopes. Cut a 3″ × ¼″

THE WITCH'S MAGIC BREWS

slot in one side of each manila envelope. Glue each envelope to the back of the activity board, lining the slots on the envelopes up with the slots on the activity board. On each envelope print the consonant found on the cauldron on the reverse side.

Laminate both sides of the activity board or cover with clear Con-Tact paper. Then carefully cut open the slots and the top opening of each envelope.

Next, cut out a number of 2″ square cards from oaktag or unlined file cards. Then cut from old workbooks a number of small pictures of objects representing the initial sounds of the 3 selected consonants. Glue a different picture on each card. Laminate the picture cards.

PROCEDURE: This activity can be used as a learning center activity, a teacher-directed activity for use with a small group, or as an activity students can work on independently and individually in their spare time.

The students sort the picture cards into the correct kettles according to the letter with which the object pictured on each card begins.

SAY: Children, today I am going to place a new activity in our letter sound learning center. The activity is named The Witch's Magic Brews.

When a witch is cooking up a batch of magic brew, what does she usually cook it in? Yes, she cooks it in a great big black pot. Does she put the pot on the stove to cook it? . . . How does she cook it? . . . That's right, she puts her pot over a fire.

(Hold up the activity board.) On our activity board our witch is cooking three different kinds of magic brew! And she is putting some very, very strange things into her kettles to make her brew!

On these cards are the things she is putting into her magic brew. Turn all of the cards picture side up. Some of the picture cards are ingredients that must go into one pot and some must go into another pot. If a card is put into the wrong kettle, the magic brew in that kettle will be ruined!

Now I will tell you how to know which item should go into which kettle. One kettle has the letter _____ printed on it. This means that any picture that begins with that letter should be put into this kettle.

The second kettle has the letter _____. Only pictures that begin with that letter can be put into that pot. The third kettle has the letter _____. Only pictures that begin with that letter can be put into that pot.

BANANAS!

PURPOSE: Letter sound relationships - initial consonants

MATERIALS: 9″ × 12″ sheet of oaktag
                  fine felt-tip markers
                  colored pencils
                  yellow construction paper
                  scissors
                  old workbooks
                  rubber cement
                  small manila envelope
                  art knife
                  laminating materials

PREPARATION: Draw 3 monkeys on a sheet of 9″ × 12″ oaktag. Color them appropriately with the pencils. Select 3 letters to be practiced. Print a different letter on each monkey. Cut bananas out of yellow construction paper. From old workbooks cut out small pictures of objects that begin with the sounds of those letters. Glue a different picture on each banana. Glue a small manila envelope on the back of the activity board. Laminate. Carefully slit open the envelope opening. Store the bananas in the envelope.

PROCEDURE: The students "feed" the bananas to the monkeys by matching the initial consonant sound of the object pictured on a banana with the monkey with the corresponding letter.

SAY: This is an activity you may work on by yourself or with a friend. The name of this activity is Bananas! On the activity board there are three monkeys. Each monkey has a different letter printed on him. In the envelope on the back of the activity board, you will find bananas. Carefully take all of the bananas out of the envelope. Each banana has a different picture on it. Pick up a banana, look at the picture on it, think of the letter sound with which that picture begins, then "feed" the banana to the monkey that has the letter that makes that sound. Of course, we can't really "feed" it to the monkey so just put the banana at his feet ready for him to eat.

     Do the same with the rest of the bananas. When you have finished the activity, carefully set it on my desk and I will check it as soon as I can. Print your name on a small piece of paper and place it on top of the activity board so that I will know who did the activity. When I check it, I will call you up and we will look at it together.

CHRISTMAS LETTERS

PURPOSE: Matching capital with lower case letters and letter sound relationships

MATERIALS: 18″ × 18″ sheet of colored railroad board or posterboard
felt-tip markers
colored railroad board or posterboard
compass
scissors
paper fastener
paper clip
laminating materials
4 game markers

PREPARATION: On the sheet of colored railroad board or posterboard, draw a
game board as illustrated. Select 4–6 consonants upon which you wish the
students to drill. Print a different selected lower case letter in each space
on the game board. Laminate the game board.

To make the spinner, cut a circle with a diameter of approximately
4″, from colored railroad board. Divide it into 4–6 pie-shaped sections,
depending upon the number of consonants selected. Print a different
capital letter in each section. The letters must be the same as selected for
the game board. Laminate the spinner. Punch a hole through the center of
the cardboard circle. Insert a paper fastener through a paper clip, then
through the hole in the circle. Bend the prongs on the paper fastener,
leaving the paper fastener loose enough that the paper clip will spin
easily.

You will also need 4 game markers.

PROCEDURE: Players place their markers on *Start*. The first player spins the
spinner and names the capital letter to which it points. He then moves his
marker forward on the game board to the first space that has the matching
lower case letter. Then he names a word that begins with that letter.

Play continues in this way.

SAY: Today we have a new game to help us practice our letters and letter
sounds. It is called Christmas Letters. The object of the game is to be the
first one to reach the Christmas tree and the presents.

Place your markers on *Start*. The first player spins the spinner. He
names the capital letter to which the spinner points. He moves his marker
forward on the game board to the first space that has the matching lower
case letter. Then he names a word that begins with that letter.

It is then the next player's turn to spin the spinner and move his
marker forward, etc.

If the player is unable to name the capital letter on the spinner, is
unable to find the corresponding lower case letter on the game board, or is
unable to name a word that begins with that letter, he must be told the
correct response. Then he must move his marker back 2 spaces from the
space indicated by the spinner.

Play proceeds in this manner. The winner is the first player to land on the last space before the Christmas tree. He then automatically slides his marker onto the Christmas tree and becomes the winner.

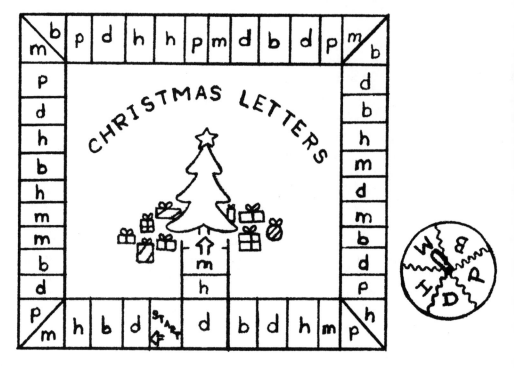

RAINDROPS

PURPOSE: Letter sound relationships

MATERIALS: unlined blue file cards or light blue construction paper
scissors
old workbooks and catalogs
rubber cement
fine felt-tip marker
laminating materials or clear Con-Tact paper
washable transparency marking pen or china marking pencil
box
attractive Con-Tact paper
paper towels

PREPARATION: Select 5–6 or more consonants upon which you want the students to drill. From old workbooks or catalogs cut out a number of different small pictures of objects to represent the initial sound of the selected consonants.

Out of unlined blue file cards or light blue construction paper, cut a number of raindrops approximately 3½″ × 2½″. (See the illustration.) Glue a different picture near the pointed end of each raindrop. Near the bottom of each raindrop draw two lines. On the two lines the students will print the capital and lower case form of the initial consonant represented by the picture on that raindrop.

Laminate all raindrops or cover with clear Con-Tact paper.

Cover a box with attractive Con-Tact paper. Store the raindrops in this box. Also place in the box a washable transparency marking pen or a china marking pencil.

PROCEDURE: The student prints the capital and lower case form of the initial consonant represented by the picture on each raindrop using the washable transparency marker or china marking pencil.

SAY: I am going to place a new box of activity cards on our activity table. They are called Raindrops because each card is in the shape of a raindrop.

Each raindrop has a picture and two lines on it. Select a raindrop. Decide with what letter the picture on that raindrop begins. Then print the capital and lower case form of the letter on the lines using this special marking pen.

Do each Raindrop in this way. When you have finished all of the raindrops, bring them to me and we will look over your answers. Then wipe your answers off each raindrop with a paper towel. Then place the Raindrops and the special marking pen back in the box and put them back on the table ready for another student to do.

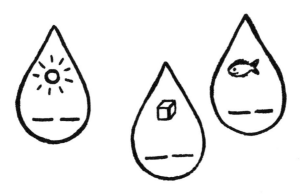

CLOTHESPIN CLIP BOARD

PURPOSE: Alphabetical order, matching capital and lower case letters, and
letter sound relationships

MATERIALS: plywood or masonite
26 spring-type clothespins
strong glue
paper cutter
13 unlined pink 3″ × 5″ file cards
13 unlined blue 3″ × 5″ file cards
old workbooks
scissors
rubber cement
unlined yellow 3″ × 5″ file cards

PREPARATION: Use strong glue to glue the clothespins on the plywood or
masonite, well-spaced in rows.

Cut the pink, blue and yellow cards in half so they each measure 1″
× 2½″. Print a different capital letter on each pink card. Print a different
lower case letter on each blue card.

From old workbooks, cut pictures to represent the beginning sound
of each letter of the alphabet. Omit a picture for X. You may wish to cut
out several pictures for each letter. Glue a different picture on each yellow
card.

Variation: Seasonal shape cards can be used instead of rectangular
cards.

PROCEDURE: The student clips the capital and the lower case letter cards on
the Clothespin Clip Board in alphabetical order. Then the student clips
each picture card behind the appropriate capital and lower case letter
cards. There is no picture card for the letter X.

SAY: This is our Clothespin Clip Board and here are sets of cards. There is a
different capital letter printed on each pink card. There is a different lower
case letter on each blue card. And there are pictures on each of the yellow
cards.

Spread out the pink capital letter cards. Find a card with capital A on
it. Clip it in the first clothespin. Then find the card with B and clip it in
the next clothespin. Clip the rest of the cards on the Clothespin Clip
Board in alphabetical order.

Then spread out the blue cards with the lower case letters. Clip them
on the board in alphabetical order, placing the lower case letter in the
clothespin with the matching capital letter card.

Next, spread out the picture cards. Pick up a picture card, think what object is pictured, decide with what letter that object begins, then clip the card *behind* the appropriate letter cards. Do the same with each picture card. There will be no picture card for X.

When you have finished, ask me to come check your work.

METHODS FOR HELPING STUDENTS
WHO HAVE GREAT DIFFICULTY

In every kindergarten and first grade class there are a couple of students who just can't seem to remember the letter names from one day to the next. Some students can't even remember the letter names from one minute to the next.

This chapter describes a method and a number of activities that can be used effectively with these students.

For students who have great difficulty learning the letter names, plan on spending a number of days teaching a single letter. And, plan on presenting that letter in a number of different ways.

When providing instruction for children who are having great difficulty learning the letters, try to work with them in *very* small groups. This shouldn't be a problem since there are usually only a couple of children in a typical class who would need this special type of presentation.

INSTRUCTIONAL PROCEDURE:

FIRST DAY:

1. Select the letter to be taught.
2. Show the student the *glue and salt tactile card* for that letter (see p. 19). Tell him the name of the letter. Take his pointer finger and index finger in your hand and guide his fingers over the letter in the correct way for printing the letter. As you do this, have him say the letter name. Help him trace his fingers over the letter several times.
3. Next, have the student practice forming the letter in the salt of the *tactile box* (see p. 19) using his pointer finger and index finger as his pencil. As he prints the letter, have him say the name of the letter aloud. Shake the salt to erase the letter. Have him repeat this step 4 times.
4. Hand him an unlined sheet of paper with the lines of the letter dotted in (see p. 28). Have him trace over the dotted lines with a crayon to form the letter in solid lines. Make sure that he forms the parts of the letter in the correct sequence and direction.

5. Next, give the student a bright colored sheet of construction paper on which the letter has been printed quite large. Have him dribble glue over the lines of the letter and place pieces of corn (or rice, cereal, or beans, etc.) along the lines to form the letter. Let him take this home at the end of the school day. (See GLUE-A-LETTER p. 30.)

SECOND DAY:

1. Show the student the tactile card of the same letter taught on the first day. Tell him the name of the letter. And have him trace over the tactile letter once with his finger tips while saying aloud the letter name. Make sure he forms the letter in the correct manner. Guide his hand only if necessary.
2. Have him print the letter in the tactile box. Let him look at the tactile card letter to see how it is formed. Have him say the letter name aloud as he forms it.
3. Give him a blob of play dough. Show him how to roll it into a "snake", then bend it around and break off pieces to form the letter (see PLAY DOUGH LETTERS, p. 21). Squash the play dough up and let him form the letter. Let the play dough letter dry for approximately 24 hours. Then let him paint his letter with water colors or tempera paint. When it is thoroughly dry, let him take the letter home.
4. Using a washable *non-toxic* magic marker, print the letter on the child's hand. (see LETTERS ON HANDS, p. 18). Whenever you walk by the child during the day, reach down, open his hand so that you both can see the letter, and ask the child the name of the letter. If he cannot remember, patiently tell him the letter name.

Note: If for any reason a parent objects to having his child's hand marked on with magic marker, discontinue this step on that child.

THIRD DAY:

1. Show the student the tactile card of the letter and tell him the letter name. Have him trace over it once with his fingers as he says the letter name aloud.
2. Next, give him an assortment of colors of chalk. Print the letter on the blackboard. Have him cover an entire section of blackboard with the letter using various colors of chalk, printing the letters in various sizes and at varying angles. (See COVER THE CHALKBOARD, p. 29.) Each time he prints the letter have him say its name softly aloud.

The student will probably have the letter mastered at this point. If so, cut a star out of yellow Con-Tact paper. Print the letter on the star with permanent black magic marker. Peel the paper backing off the star. Stick the star onto the student's shirt as an award showing that the student has learned that letter.

The student should be presented with a new letter to learn the next day.

If the student has not mastered the letter by the end of the lesson on the third day, proceed onto the fourth day activities.

FOURTH DAY:

1. Show the student the tactile card of the letter and tell him the letter name. Have him trace over it once with his fingers as he says the letter name aloud.

2. Give him some finger paint and a sheet of finger paint paper. Let him print the letter over and over again in finger paint. Have him say aloud the name of the letter each time he prints it. Have him use his pointer finger and index finger as his "pencil". Have him erase the letter by rubbing his hand gently over the paper. Then have him print the letter again.

   After about 5 minutes, have him make the letter one more time, making it the neatest he can. Allow to dry. Then let the student take it home.

3. Have the student make a LETTER SEARCH POSTER. Give him a large sheet of construction paper and some old magazines and newspapers. Have him cut out that letter each time he finds it. Young children should cut out the larger size letters found in titles and advertizements. Some of the small print letters would be too small for them to handle. Have him glue the letters on the construction paper to make an attractive poster. Hang this poster up in the classroom for several days. Then let him take it home.

ACTIVITIES FOR FURTHER INSTRUCTION

The following activities are appropriate if further instructional activities for the letter are needed:

When teaching the next letter, use the general procedure just outlined. However, any of the 5 activities listed above can be used as alternatives to the activities in the four day program to add variety and maintain the child's interest.

When 4–6 letters have been learned, begin to provide games, activities, and review to help the child maintain that knowledge. Limit the letters in the activity, game or on the gameboard to the letters the child has learned.

COMMERCIAL INSTRUCTIONAL MATERIALS

The following lists some of the commercial instructional materials available on the alphabet.

Arista Corporation 2440 Estand Way P. O. Box 6146 Concord, CA 94524	ALPHA TIME
Developmental Learning Materials 7400 Natchez Avenue Niles, IL 60648	LETTER CONSTANCY CARDS ALPHABET MATCHING FLIP BOOK ALPHA-TRACKS
Edu-Cards Binney and Smith P.O. Box 431 Easton, PA 18042	ABC LOTTO LETTER RECOGNITION GAME LEARNING THE ALPHABET ALPHABET
ESP, Inc. 1201 E. Johnson P. O. Drawer 5037 Jonesboro, AR 72401	ALPHABET (duplicator book) MANUSCRIPT (duplicator book)
Guidance Industries Dept. 1, Box 247 61 Camino Alto Mill Valley, CA 94941	ALPHABLOCKS
Hayes School Publishing Co. 321 Pennwood Avenue Wilkinsburg, PA 15221	LET'S WRITE SERIES, BOOK I (manuscript)
Ideal School Supply Company 1100 S. Lavergne Avenue Oal Lawn, IL 60453	FLOCKED ALPHABET WALL CARDS BLACK AND WHITE BEADED ALPHABET CARDS COLOR BEADED ALPHABET CARDS

BEADED ALPHABET CHART
FELT LETTERS (for flannel boards)
CUT-OUT LETTERS AND
    NUMERALS
GROOVY LETTERS
ALPHABET PRACTICE CARDS
FROGGIE ALPHABET GAME
SPIDER CRAWL
ALPHABET DESK CARDS

Instructo/McGraw-Hill
Paoli, PA 19301

MAGNETIC LETTERS
KINESTHETIC TRACE-THE-LETTER
    CARDS
WOODEN LETTERS
FLANNELBOARD LETTERS
LEARNING CENTERS—FUN WITH
    CAPITAL AND LOWER CASE
    LETTERS
DESK TAPE MANUSCRIPT LETTER
    LINE
KNOW 'N SHOW ALPHABET
WALK-ON-SETS STEPPING
    STONES ALPHABET
    CAPITALS
WALK-ON-SETS STEPPING
    STONES ALPHABET LOWER
    CASE
ALPHABET EXPRESS (wall chart)
ALPHABET STORYLAND (wall chart)
MY ALPHABET TRAIN
LEARNING TO FORM ALPHABET
    LETTERS
LETTER RECOGNITION

Instructor Curriculum Materials
Dansville, NY 14437

ALPHABET RECOGNITION
    (duplicator book)
ALPHABETICAL ORDER
    (duplicator book)

Judy Company
310 N. School St.
Minneapolis, MN 55401

LETTER AND NUMERAL SET

Kenworthy P.O. Box 60 Buffalo, NY 14205	CUT OUT LETTERS
Kleeco	KLEECO'S CHALK "REMARK- ABLE" BOOKS: ALPHA PRINT BOOK—BASIC ALPHA PRINT BOOK—AD- VANCED KLEECO'S JUNIOR "RE-MARKABLE" PRINTING BOOK
Lauri, Inc. Phillips-Avon, ME 04966	ALPHABET AVALANCHE (1000 rubber letters) ALPHASET LETTERS (rubber letters) RUBBER PICTURE PUZZLES JUMBO ALPHA-A-NUMBER A TO Z PANELS ALPH-A-SPACE
J. B. Lippincott Company East Washington Square Philadelphia, PA 19105	BEGINNING TO READ, WRITE AND LISTEN
McGraw Hill/Early Learning Manchester Rd. Manchester, MO 63011	LEARNING TO FORM CONSONANT LETTERS, SPIRIT DUPLICATING MASTERS BOOK LEARNING TO FORM LETTERS SPIRIT DUPLICATING MASTERS BOOK
Manderite, Inc. P.O. Box 202 Allenhurst, NJ 07711	MANDERITE KINESTHETIC TRACING ALPHABET KINESTHETIC TRACING ALPHABET IN SHEET FORM SIMPLICATED WRITING BOARDS
Matell Inc. 5150 Rosecrans Avenue Hawthorne, CA 90250	THE BEE SAYS SEE 'N SAY TOY

Milton Bradley
1500 Main Street
Springfield, MA 01105
	ALPHABET WALL CARDS
	GIANT ALPHABET POSTER CARDS
	ALPHABET PUZZLE CARDS—
	    MANUSCRIPT
	FLANNEL BOARD MANUSCRIPT
	    LETTERS
	LOWER CASE CARDBOARD
	    LETTERS
	LEARN TO WRITE LETTER
	    CARDS—MANUSCRIPT

Playskool, Inc. 4501 W. Augusta Chicago, IL 60651	MAGNETIC LETTERS ALPHABET PUZZLE BOARD KINESTHETIC ALPHABET
Selchow and Righter Co. 200 Fifth Avenue New York, NY 10010	SCRABBLE—ALPHABET GAME

Singer/Society for Visual Education
1345 Diversey Parking
Chicago, IL 60614
	MOTIVATOR ACTIVITY CARDS—
	    FOLLOW THE DOTS
	    ALPHABET
	MOTIVATOR ACTIVITY CARDS—
	    MANUSCRIPT WRITING
	    CARDS

Trend Enterprises Inc.
P. O. Box 43073
St. Paul, MN 55164
	PUNCH-A-SHAPE ALPHABET
	BULLETIN BOARD TABLET
	    GAMES—THE ALPHABET
	ALPHABET PARADE
	WIPE-OFF CARDS—
	    THE ALPHABET
	WIPE-OFF CARDS A–Z DOT TO DOT
	WIPE-OFF CARDS MANUSCRIPT
	    ALPHABET
	ALPHABET BINGO
	PUNCH THROUGH CARDS—
	    INITIAL CONSONANTS
	PUNCH THROUGH CARDS—
	    FINAL CONSONANTS
	THE ALPHABET FLIP BOOK

Child Guidance Toy Div.
1055 Bronx River Avenue
Bronx, NY 10472

MAGNETIC ALPHABET AND
    SPELLING BOARD
GIANT MAGNETIC ALPHABET
    AND CHALK BOARD
MAGNETIC LETTERS